Thank you!

Be Bless and Enjoy!

Dr. Frazier Ben Todd, Sr.

Blessed *from the* Beginning

The Remarkable Life of Dr. Frazier Ben Todd, Sr.

(As told to Janice Jerome)

A Physician, Pastor & Retired Major from Atlanta, Georgia

Dr. Frazier Ben Todd, Sr.

Janice Jerome, MPA, RP, PG, Mediator

Compiler, Interviewer and Team Leader of the Todd-Smith Project:
Janice Jerome, MPA, BS, RJP, PG, Mediator

ISBN: 978-1-54396-209-3

Todd-Smith Project Team:
Original Transcriber of Taped Interviews: Cynthia Walker
Original Proof: Dr. Amanda Strickland Hayes
Editing Reader 1: Kim Dixon
Editing Reader 2: Silent Contributor

First Edition, January 2019
Library of Congress Cataloging-in Publication Data.

Printed in the United States of America

Pictures found in this book are from Dr. Todd's albums. Other family and friends also contributed. The back-cover picture of Dr. Todd and a patient is from public domain. Naming all my family, friends, colleagues and acquaintances that have been a blessing in my life would require me to begin another book in order to list them all. I would love to hear from everyone via email.
Please send your email to drfbtsr@yahoo.com.

Dedication

This book is dedicated to the ancestors and descendants of Dr. Frazier Ben Todd, Sr.

Epigraph

"If there is light in the soul,
There will be beauty in the person.
If there is beauty in the person
There will be harmony in the house.
If there is harmony in the house,
There will be order in the nation.
If there is order in the nation,
There will be peace in the world."

Old Chinese Proverb

FOREWORD

My father, Dr. Frazier Ben Todd, Sr., is my mentor and role model. I chose my career path in medicine due to my exposure from working with him when I was younger. As an adult, I understand the person my father is and who he had to become, and how his life and the experiences he faced shaped him to be the man he is today.

I am amazed at my father's accomplishments. He was born in the Deep South in Georgia and was the son of a sharecropper. He was raised on a farm where the bathroom was an outhouse and every room had a chamber pot. He was born at a time when the television was just invented and water for the home was drawn from a well. He grew up in a time where most roads consisted of red dirt and a gritty, slurry of sand and gravel, not smooth concrete with yellow-striped lines. He grew up in a time where horses still shared the roads with cows and chickens. To some, this may sound like a very distant time in history, but for my father, this was the beginning. It was the beginning of a man who was born into a segregated world where he was told he was not an equal. It was a time when he was told that he did not and would never have full rights as a citizen. The laws and society of the time where structured to make sure black men like my father failed at everything and anything they attempted. He was told to accept the status quo, to sit on the back of the bus, to walk to the back of the restaurant, and he endured mental, physical, and verbal oppression. These were the beginnings of Frazier Ben Todd, Sr., a black man who could never pass for anything but a black man. His skin was too black, too dark, his nose was too big and his hair too coarse.

And from this humble, poor neighborhood in segregated Atlanta, a man began his life and set out a plan to become educated with book sense and life sense. Whatever obstacles crossed his path, he would have the knowledge and physical tools to make the necessary actions to define his own life. This man, my father, continues to make his own path. This book could not capture all his accomplishments and struggles. Nevertheless, I appreciate and love him for having the courage to share intimate portions of his life. We cannot wait for the next book.

Love you, Dad.

Tobi Todd, DPM

May 1, 2016
Atlanta, Georgia

Dr. Frazier Ben Todd, Sr., with son Tobi Todd, DPM, Atlanta, GA

ACKNOWLEDGEMENTS

This book would not exist without the help of the Todd-Smith Project Team.

Words of Hope from Dr. Frazier Ben Todd, Sr.

It is my hope that the reader will be able to travel with me with the words I have penned of experiences in my life. This journey started at my birth and continues until my present adult life. My story is not over. I wish to be an inspiration to the readers in their own lives.

This short biography is not a full reflection of my experiences, yet they reflect a significant and meaningful portion of my life. This biography was not intended to be in chronological order of my life story. I had many flashbacks and the memories come to mind when writing down the story of my life. The memories were not always in order. I had to just get the stories out. Some chapters overlap with experiences from a child to young teenager. I was married three times and lessons and experiences are shared from past and present emotion. There are no linear paths in my writing.

I have enjoyed penning my experiences; I hope sharing my reflections will touch you in a positive way. May God bless you and may the Spirit of Life give you hope, peace, tranquility and faith that you too, with God's help be able to realize your dreams.

Be Blessed!
Dr. Frazier Ben Todd, Sr.

INTRODUCTION

I am authoring my story to inspire future generations to reach for the sky and to touch the universe. This book came into being because I realized that my family genealogy needed to be clearly documented and shared. I am excited about the research that provided me with information on my ancestors as well as descendants such as their name, date of birth, date of death, where they lived, their occupation, military background as well as census information on their community, neighbors and in some instances their social security numbers. This book has allowed me to discover how my childhood and adult experiences, were remarkably like many African American men of my age group. Growing up in the 1940's and 1950's in the segregated South (Georgia), were full of love, pain, challenges, and excitement. I also realize that my struggles are still relevant in this futuristic, technological world that we live in today. I am honored to be able to share my story, which was not about opportunities as much as it was about reaching my destiny. I am blessed to be a father, husband, serviceman, physician, and pastor.

Additionally, penning my story, *Blessed from the Beginning*, is to encourage those with similar past experiences to have hope for a brighter future, and to share with my descendants and others my deeply rooted family values. I was blessed with the privilege of having parents who showed extraordinary strength, religious ethics and served as a good family support system for me and my siblings.

I was born in the metro Atlanta area and I love Atlanta. I would not want to live anywhere else in the world. It's a place of my choice now. After living and working in many places, God had directed me back home to Atlanta—the home of the free, the home of the Atlanta Braves, the home of the Atlanta Falcons, and the home in which I will be buried. This is my place, my home.

I entered the US Armed forces in 1958, started practicing medicine in 1973, and entered the ministry in 1977. My civilian, military, and ministry educational experiences have provided me the ability to be creative and seek many educational fields to grow and be consistent in my professional development. The military brought me an intellectual growth that I was able to transfer, with committed determination, to my civilian life. My family values allowed me to achieve even higher goals in my medical career and in the ministry, which was the anchor of my soul and spirit.

I have faced challenging times with my family, career, and society, and at the same time I have been fortunate enough to reach many goals successfully. I have been honored for many accomplishments and lead many causes. I salute my wife and ex-wives for their contributions to my growth. Nancy, my first love, Terumi, my second love, and Roberta, my final love, all allowed me to continue my professional education without hindrance. Nancy was there for me when I joined the military and attended college. Terumi was there for me in my medical schooling with the army, my early private practice, and basic ministry calling. Roberta has enhanced my private medical career and life as a pastor and leader in the community. All three women have been my strongest supporters.

I hope that readers will understand that life is a continuous circle. When you stay in the circle, you will achieve many of your goals. The circle does not have a period, a comma, a question mark, or an exclamation point. Just keep each day in focus and travel within this space. The space is the dash between the day of your birth and the date you transition back to God. Please be blessed as you read these words that capture a part of my life story. – Dr. Frazier Ben Todd, Sr.

(Please Note: Dr. Frazier Ben Todd, Sr., co-authored this book. Please know that information contained in this book covers eighty years of Dr. Todd's lifespan and are true to the best of Dr. Todd's memory. There may be information that may not be totally exact especially with dates, spellings, and locations.)

CONTENTS

Foreword vii

Acknowledgements ix

Introduction x

Chapter 1 The Beginning - Riverdale, Georgia 1

Chapter 2 Home Remedies 15

Chapter 3 Lasting Memories from Childhood 19

Chapter 4 Concerned and Frightened 23

Chapter 5 The Joy of Living - Moving to Turner Way 25

Chapter 6 The Pre-Teen Years 31

Chapter 7 A Black Boy in the Deep South 34

Chapter 8 Family Foundation 43

Chapter 9 Deeply Rooted 58

Chapter 10 Coming of Age 72

Chapter 11 A Heavy Loss 79

Chapter 12 My First Love, Nancy 82

Chapter 13 Active Military Duty - (1958-1967) 100

Chapter 14 Medical School - After Military Career 121

Chapter 15 My Second Love, Terumi 128

Chapter 16 My Life as a Bachelor - San Francisco 144

Chapter 17 My Third Love, Roberta 149

Chapter 18 Podiatric Surgeon 163

Chapter 19 A Time to Share 180

Chapter 20 My Faith 183

Chapter 21 The Journey Home 188

Chapter 22 Blessed from the Beginning 199

Message From the Children of Dr. Frazier Ben Todd, Sr. 201

Biography 203

Dr. Frazier Ben Todd, Sr., Timeline 208

About the Co-Author, Janice Jerome 213

CHAPTER 1
THE BEGINNING

Riverdale, Georgia

I was born on April 4, 1939, in Riverdale, Georgia. My mother, Mary Alice Smith, told me that I was born on a Thursday at midnight, but according to my birth certificate, I was born on a Tuesday in the early morning in Clayton County, Georgia. According to data that I researched later in life online, it was a rainy day. I am sure it did not make much difference to Mom. She said "She was just happy I had arrived."

I always knew that when I grew up I wanted to do something outstanding. I did not realize as a child my desire for more meant I had to be secure financially, spiritually, mentally, and socially; then I could travel around the world. I did not look at things as rich or poor because I did not know I grew up poor until I was an adult. However, what I really wanted was to live a fulfilled, enriched life helping and healing others. I am happy to say that I have accomplished all of that, and more.

I grew up in a large family. My parents, Floyd Henry Todd and Mary Alice Smith, had nine children together. Mary Alice was my father's third wife. My mother Mary Alice had one child, my brother Nathaniel before she married my father. The firstborn out of the union of my parents was Lee Ernest. Ernest was followed by Charlie and then Richard. Mom did not think she would ever give birth to a girl; what a surprise with Thelma!

I came next, as the fifth-born. The next was Joan. After that, there was a stillbirth, Willie James. Then she had Larry, Mattie Jean, and Carolyn.

I had other brothers and sisters by my dad's first wife, Idona. They were Henry, Betsy Ann, Elease, Eddie, George, and Melvina (Viney).

Additionally, I had brothers and sisters by my Dad's second wife, Ola. Their children together were Viola, Robert, and Ruth. Life was always busy!

Growing up in the local Atlanta area enriched my life. My family moved to several homes during my childhood within the Thomasville community. I have wonderful memories of all of them. The first house I grew up in was in Riverdale, Georgia. It was an old house. We lived on a "route box," which is a designated mail delivery in rural areas. Our house did not have an address. Around age two years old, I remember the wood burning in the fireplace, and the bricks it was standing on, creating a crawl space underneath.

During World War II, my dad, Floyd, worked at the Bell Bomber Plant, which some may remember as Lockheed Air force Base in Marietta, Georgia. It is presently known as Dobbins Air Reserve Base. We moved from Riverdale to the suburbs of unincorporated Atlanta (Fulton County), to a community called Thomasville, around 1941 or 1942.

My Second Home: Phillips Drive

The family's second house was in Thomasville, at 708 Phillips Drive. I was around three years old at the time. The house had different rooms of various sizes. There was a wood-burning stove in the kitchen and a wood-burning stove for general heat, because we did not have electricity or running water for any type of furnace. We used an outhouse, and had to carry water from the well to the house. This home was also built on bricks. As children, we played many different games under the house in inclement weather, including hide-and-seek. When Mom was looking for us, she would always start looking under the house. Whenever it was really storming, we had to go into the house, because tornadoes were quite common in the South.

When we lived in the house on Phillips Drive, there were thirteen siblings: Ruth, Viola, Nathaniel, Lee Ernest, Charlie, Richard, Thelma, Joan, Mattie Jean, Larry, Carol, and myself, all living with my parents, Floyd and Mary. However, some of my siblings were in the military or had relocated from Atlanta to New York. I do not recall the number of bedrooms, but I remember there were eight boys in one room and all the girls shared a room. The living room and dining room were sleeping quarters, and the babies always slept in the same room as Mom and Dad.

My Earliest Childhood Memory

My earliest childhood memory was of an incident that happened when I was two years old. Our house had a fireplace and a hearth. It was a cold winter night, and we were all sitting around the fireplace eating peanuts. I recall that my dad was shaving.

My mother and father had disciplined me to go around the hearth and not run across the fireplace. However, that night, I ran across the fireplace and fell. I hit the pot of boiling water that was hanging over the fireplace. The water spilled out of the pot, burning my arms and upper chest. Mom yelled in panic and bolted out of her chair, then grabbed my legs to pull me out of the fire. As I screamed from the pain, Mom placed homemade herbal remedies on my injuries before wrapping me up with cloth. My mother did everything right that night because I was in good shape from her care. The scars on my arms and chest from the burn are a reminder of that day so long ago.

After my burn incident, one of my oldest brothers, Richard, became one of my first teachers. Richard was four years older than I was. One time, I was trying to bite a hickory nut to open it, and Richard said, "Frazier, that's not how you open a hickory nut." So, began one of the many lessons of brotherly love. Richard showed me how to use two rocks to open a hickory nut—one rock to lay the hickory on, and the other rock to hit the hickory. We sat there eating hickory nuts and enjoying each other. It was a great lesson!

Growing up on Phillips Drive

Living in our home on Phillips Drive, we did not have the luxurious amenities and other necessities of today. Our home did not have a refrigerator; instead, we had an icebox. The iceman—I believe his name was Jack—would come at least twice a week and bring us ice. We did not have electricity in the house, so my parents would buy one hundred pounds of ice, which would last us three or four days, so we had to be incredibly careful how we used it. The ice froze meats and foods like vegetables from the family garden. The ice was kept in the top of the icebox.

Furthermore, our house on Phillips Drive was situated on a hill; there was plenty of space to roam around. Our house was built around the well, which was in the backyard uphill from the outhouse. The water we drank from the well was clean per the state health department. The outhouse was the family's outdoor bathroom and was located about three hundred feet downhill from the well. We always kept the well clean and clear from the outhouse. Dad made sure snails were not in the well; he would put salt into the well to keep them away.

One of the more distinctive features was the hog pens. We had twenty to thirty-five hogs at any given time. Dad would separate the hogs when he got ready to slaughter them. He would put aside two or three hogs and fatten them for the family's meat later in the wintertime. As a young child I did not understand the process or his purpose, until I was older. The neighbors always came to help my father kill the hogs and the meat would be shared with the neighbors. The rest of the meat was placed in our smokehouse. The smokehouse was also located in the backyard, inside a separate structure. Dad would hang meat from the ceiling in the smokehouse.

Our family also had a cow named Daisy. Daisy lived in the barn. She gave us all the milk we needed. We had cornbread and buttermilk every day, and we used the icebox to preserve the milk. When I was around seven years old, my brother Richard taught me how to milk the cow properly. I had to pull the cow nipples from the top and squeeze from the bottom with my thumb and index finger. I pulled and squeezed all the way down. If I did not do it right, Daisy would kick me. She would glare at me and wave her tail around my head. I have had my fair share of feeling her cow tail over the years.

Growing up, we had a dog-named Jack. Jack was a big, brown dog with long ears. A family friend gave him to the family as a puppy. Jack played with us and slept under the house as a watchdog. All my brothers said that Jack loved each of them.

He was their favorite dog because Jack did what my brothers and sisters told him to do. Jack was around for ten years, and then he died of old age. I helped bury him in the back yard at our home on Phillips Drive.

I loved animals—our dog, cow, and pigs—but we also had to be careful of dangerous animals. Our parents always warned us to be careful of poisonous snakes and to never approach a snake. Georgia has its fair share of poisonous snakes—rattlesnakes, copperheads, and cottonmouths, to name a few.

Toys and Games

As a child, I had some toys and games that I would play with and enjoy with my family and friends. My favorite toys were my BB gun and a cap pistol (a toy gun that creates a loud sound like a gunshot) with little caps that would shoot repeatedly. My brothers, friends, and I played cowboys and Indians in the woods. For the horse, we would wrap different cloths around a stick. Sometimes I would be Tonto (Indian who was the Lone Ranger's partner) and someone else would be the Lone Ranger (masked man -western hero). The others would be the Indians and the sheriff.

When I was around seven years old, I played a game called "punch a car." When my friends and I saw a car, we claimed the car as our own. We knew the names of every car. You could look at a car and know if it was a Hudson Motor Car, Chrysler, Edison, Chevrolet, or a Ford. The automobile industry has since stopped manufacturing many of the older models. Other boys from the neighborhood and I would stand on the highway bank and call out, "That's my car!"

As a child, I had a lot of heroes and role models. My heroes were baseball players, particularly Jackie Robinson, because I was not aware of any famous African-American football players at that time. I looked up to George Washington Carver because he was a scientist, as well as other black heroes, like Booker T. Washington, who was a great educator and founder of the Tuskegee University. My favorite TV show was Amos 'n' Andy. Amos 'n' Andy was an American radio and television show set in Harlem, the black mecca of the north. I enjoyed the television show that aired once a week. I thought the actors did an excellent job and it was good comedy.

Over an Acre of Land

We had a big yard on about two acres of land in our second home on Phillips Drive. We played hopscotch in the yard and played on a hill on the side of the house that we called "Red Dirt Hill." I have many fond memories of playing on Red Dirt Hill.

Reverend Odom lived in our neighborhood. He would bring his mule and wagon to our home on Phillips Drive to prepare the garden for Dad. Reverend Odom was responsible for plowing and turning our soil over in preparation for the seeding and planting of corn, sweet potatoes, and other vegetables. He often allowed my brother Richard and me to try to plow a row or two. Of course, we would mess up because we were unable to hold the plow in the soil to keep the rows straight. After our attempts, he would come and straighten the rows out.

Mom had a half-acre of land set aside for her gardens. There was a big cornfield and a sweet potato patch; there were beans, okra, tomatoes, and other vegetables that served us well.

We had vegetables all year round because Mom would preserve and canned them. There was also a big tree in our yard. One tree is presently located where Mount Nebo Baptist Church is in Thomasville. We had a big swing in that tree, and we would climb up and swing. I had lots of fun there.

Sweet Potato Hill

One of the funniest family stories involved a sweet potato hill when I lived on Phillips Drive. Our sweet potato hill was when my siblings and I pulled up all the sweet potatoes that had been planted the previous season and turned them over. We always laid them out to dry, with a certain percentage of those sweet potatoes placed aside to be eaten. Dirt and straw would be placed around the sweet potatoes so the potatoes could be eaten later and would not become spoiled in cold weather. The sweet potatoes would stay at a certain temperature. I did not really know how it worked at the time, but I know now that it has something to do with the soil maintaining moisture. I was always concerned that there was going to be a snake in the dirt when I pulled out the sweet potatoes.

Our family had sweet potatoes almost all year round. We would take two big baskets of sweet potatoes and bury them in the sweet potato hill. We would go out, get some sweet potatoes, bring them in, and roast them in the fireplace. One of my weaknesses was sweet potato custard. Mom told me, "Son, that's your birthmark, because when I was carrying you I could not get enough sweet potatoes."

Dad made sure that he always had some sweet potatoes for Mom to bake or cook. Dad would tease Mom because of her love for sweet potatoes. He would say, "Mary Alice, when you die and go to heaven, everyone else will be asking God for wings, but you're going to ask God if he has any sweet potatoes," and then all the children would laugh.

Grade School

I remember our house on Phillips Drive was on a dirt road located about five or six blocks from where we went to church, Mount Carmel African Methodist Episcopal Church (AME). I have great memories of that church. The schoolhouse, Thomasville Elementary, was located next to the church. My parents joined Mount Carmel in the early 1940s and I was baptized at around six years old.

I went to grade school at Thomasville Elementary School. The first time I was in a classroom setting was when I entered the first grade. I had never been so excited. My teacher for first and second grade, Mrs. Madison, was the smartest woman in the world-other than my mom-because Mrs. Madison knew so much.

It was a time for me to learn, but I also enjoyed spending time with my friends. I was a decent student and liked most subjects, but in my opinion, as I progressed to later grades in elementary school there was nothing as difficult as geography.

For some reason, geography was so challenging for me. I had a difficult time remembering the names of cities and finding the United States on the map. I had a gift for mathematics though. Working with numbers never gave me any trouble. Aaron, a young kid in the neighborhood, was also gifted in math. We were good friends in school, and always in competition to receive the highest grade on tests. We did not have preschool or kindergarten, but when I was promoted to the first grade, I already knew how to read. The teacher used flash cards for the words I already knew. I enjoyed school and found that it was easy.

When my siblings and I would come home from school, we all sat around a big table to do homework. There were two lamps, one at each end of the table. My older brothers and sisters would do their homework while Mom would read to the younger siblings. I always enjoyed that time of day because we were all together.

The schoolhouse had four rooms. The first –and second-graders were in one room, the third-and fourth-graders were in another room, the fifth-and sixth graders were in another room, and the seventh graders were in a room by themselves.

The Community Church

My faith was a big part of my life growing up and even into adulthood. Many of the families in the community knew each other, and we rarely locked our doors. The church was unlocked; you could go to the church to just sit down, or rest, meditate, and pray, whatever you wanted to do. There were three churches in Thomasville: Mount NEBO Baptist Church, Mount Carmel AME Church, and Bible Way Church. There was also a community named Macedonia that was located on Jonesboro Road, which was just southwest of Thomasville. Their elementary school went to the sixth grade and then they would come to the Thomasville community for the seventh grade. Only a few students from Macedonia would graduate with us.

Contributing to the Family

Outside of school, we worked to help the family. We did not get an allowance because we worked for everything we had. If we did not already have a job, we had an opportunity each summer to find employment.

Periodically, when I was six, I worked for Milton Baker as a carboy. Thomasville was rural. Mr. Baker could not drive the route and throw the paper, so he would drive and I would run up and put the paper on the porch. I made a dollar a day; five dollars a week, great for a six-year-old. I learned early that work could be enjoyable and was happy to contribute to my family.

World Events

As a young child, the big world events that affected my life were World War II and the events surrounding the times. The tears of the adults in my community made me realize the importance of the death of our leaders in society. I remember when President Franklin D. Roosevelt (FDR) died in 1945. The train carrying his remains traveled from Warm Springs in Georgia through Atlanta, Georgia, to Washington, DC. People were lined up along the railroad tracks and watched as the train with FDR's remains passed. I remember the sadness in the eyes of my community members.

The United States victory of World War II was a major development during my life. In 1945, the United States dropped two atomic bombs on two Japanese cities, Hiroshima and Nagasaki, and then Japan surrendered. That was one of the greatest events as we celebrated the surrender of Japan, but I did not understand at the time that this weapon could destroy the whole world.

Many people in my community had relatives and friends who were overseas fighting in the war. As a child, I remember Mom and Dad praying for my brothers George, Robert, and Nathaniel, who were in the military. The only exemption from the draft was if you were the only male child or had a disability that prevented you from serving. My brothers and I all served in the military—George, Robert, and Nathaniel served in World War II, Charlie served in post-Korea, Richard served in pre-Vietnam, and I served in the Vietnam theater of operations and Operation Desert Storm.

One image that stayed with me was that of the Western Union truck driving throughout the community of Thomasville. When the truck came into the area, I knew that one of our men from our community sustained injury or had been killed. I remember the sound of women screaming when the Western Union truck drove up. One day, we were sitting on the porch and the Western Union truck came by, but he did not stop. I will never forget the look on Mom's face—a mix of panic and sadness and shock. Then Mom sighed with relief once the truck continued to another place.

I remember as a young child sitting on the hills overlooking Moreland Avenue watching the soldiers drive by in the big Army trucks, jeeps, cars, and other military vehicles. It gave me such a great thrill. I wanted to travel and see the world, just like those soldiers. That was during the years of World War II.

World War II ended in 1945, when I was six years old. I was eleven when the next major event started, the Korean War. It was devastating because many family friends from my community lost their lives in active duty, never to return home. I understood the effects of the war because my family would discuss the death of those who did not return and the many funerals that were occurring in the community. My niece, Rosa Todd Water's, father Sergeant William Herndon, US Army NCOIC, suffered severe wounds in the Korean war.

Floyd Henry Todd approximately 20-25 years old, picture taken in Georgia around 1910.

Mary Alice Smith Todd, (1950's). Atlanta, Georgia

Mary Alice

Mary Alice Smith Todd in her early 20's

CHAPTER 2
HOME REMEDIES

Playing Outside

Being injured was just a part of being a kid. One time, when I was ten years old, I was playing outside without my shoes on. I cut my foot wide open in the woods after stepping on glass. My brothers Richard and Charlie wrapped it up with some leaves or something, and I had to limp to our family home on Phillips Drive. Mom put a piece of fatback bacon on it, wrapped it up, and said, "You'll be all right." I have a scar there now. We did not know what a podiatrist was. We rarely saw any type of a doctor. Mom took care of those things.

Getting Sick

Getting sick was a serious thing back then, but my parents always took care of us. The mumps and measles were serious and life-threatening childhood diseases in those days, before vaccines and preventative care. I remember when I was about ten years old I had the mumps. Mom tied cod liver oil, fish sauce, onions, and sardines around my neck. It was a home remedy treatment for mumps, measles, and colds.

The neighborhood I grew up in was awesome. I would not take anything in exchange for the memories of my childhood. It was so much fun and we had a great time! As I mentioned, we were poor, but not in spirit. There was a creek in the woods that ran off Phillips Drive near Moreland Avenue. The creek was another one of our hangout places. One time, we caught a snake that was about four or five feet long. It was not poisonous; it was probably a king snake. When my brothers and I brought the snake home, Mom was livid. She threatened to shoot all of us, including the snake. We took a picture of the snake wrapped around Charlie's arm. Mom wanted the snake out of the house, so we had to let the snake go. We turned it loose in the woods because we did not want to kill it.

Snakes Do Bite!

Our parents always warned my siblings and me that if a snake bit us, we could die. One day, my sister Joan, who was two years younger than me, had a bite on her leg from a snake. Joan was eight and I was ten at the time. She was somewhere between the house and the outhouse. Joan rushed into the house with her leg swollen and painful. Mom quickly sanitized the wound and wrapped it, then called the doctor; one of the rare occasions when she thought, she needed extra help. When the doctor came to the house and examined her, he determined that it was a snakebite. Mom had done everything appropriately to save Joan's life prior to the arrival of the doctor, as she had done with my burn wounds.

The reason I am alive today is by the Grace of God, despite all the things I did as a child. Mom and Dad's prayers were to protect naive, curious children. Including the time Charlie broke his arm after falling out of a tree, and my sister Joan was bitten by a snake.

Mary Alice Smith Todd home in Atlanta, approximately 1975

Frazier Todd, Sr., (with hat on) with childhood friends

Frazier Sr.'s brother Charlie holding a snake

CHAPTER 3
LASTING MEMORIES FROM CHILDHOOD

The Best Bike in the World!

Growing up left many lasting memories. When I was ten years old, my brother Charlie bought the first bicycle in our family. Charlie was sixteen years old at the time and had worked for several months. I do not know what his job was, but one night he brought home a new, shiny bicycle. I thought the bicycle was the prettiest bike I had ever seen. It was blue, as I recall.

Richard, Charlie, and I took it out for a ride that night on Moreland Avenue, one of the main highways, US 23 (before the Starlight Drive-In Theater opened). We were riding down the highway with one front light that was battery-operated, built on the fender of the front of the bicycle. I was riding shotgun on the handlebars, Charlie was pedaling, and Richard was on the back fender. Wow, what a sight! Cars drove past, honking at us, but we did not care. There was a light on our bicycle, and there were little flap tails on the side that we called "screaming eagles."

That bike brought our family much entertainment, but it also caused some strife. I was a tattletale, plain and simple. I was the sixteenth child on my dad's side and the sixth child on my mother's side. Each sibling had a different personality. I had a habit of following rules. Mom sent me with my older brothers to keep track of them because the bike was a major form of transportation for my brothers and me. Everyone knew if my siblings did something stupid, I would tell Mom.

The Cupboard

Thomasville was a fun place to grow up. There was a swimming hole we called the "Cupboard." The Cupboard was a big waterhole from a local ravine that was blocked with rocks. The Cupboard was about twenty feet wide and thirty feet long, and it was located under the railroad tracks. The Cupboard served us well in the summertime. There was a deep and shallow part for our local recreational use.

I learned how to swim (around six years old) with confidence across the shallow part. We were young girls and boys and did not have bathing suits, so all of us—boys and girls—would go skinny-dipping in the Cupboard.

We spent our summers doing our favorite thing: swimming in the Cupboard in Thomasville. However, the black community had one public park, Washington Park, which was located near Washington High School on the west side of Atlanta. When we went swimming there, we had to wear bathing suits.

The rules at Washington Park were quite strict. I believe it was five or ten cents to go swimming. When we could afford to go we had to wear bathing suits. Lifeguards were always available. Then, they built another park in the southeast section of town called Pittman Park, which was in the Pittsburgh community of Atlanta. We had a lot of fun!

We also threw rocks into the water to run the snakes out. We would make noises and watch in fascination as the snakes—water moccasins—jumped out of the water. Then we would jump in and go swimming. However, one day, one snake remained in the water, swimming between my legs. Crazy me, I tried to catch him. One of my brothers said, "Don't do that, Frazier! Let him go!" and I did.

Loving Parents

I had everything I needed growing up, from clothing, to toys, to a roof over my head and food in my belly. I had a two-piece suit to wear on Sunday and an informal day suit. I had two pairs of shoes—a pair of brown Brogan shoes (sturdy leather high top shoes), and a pair of black shoes. I went barefoot in the summertime, and that was all I needed. If new clothing, shoes, or any such item came in, it was passed down from the next sibling. I wore short pants in the summer and overalls in the winter with patches sewn onto the holes and rips. Today, kids purposely buy clothing with holes in them for fashion. Back in my day, we did not buy clothes with holes in them.

My siblings and I never had to go to the police or enter into the legal system. My mom and dad communicated excellently, because whatever Mom said was what happened. Dad was the leader of the house, but we knew that Mom was sort of the ruler. What I mean is that both Mom and Dad worked together as a team. Mom disciplined us, helped us with homework, arranged our study time, and did household chores of cooking, sewing, washing, etc.

My siblings and I were lucky. We grew up in a loving home with parents who loved each other and us unconditionally. I cherish those memories.

CHAPTER 4
CONCERNED AND FRIGHTENED

Laid out on the Road

When I was around eleven years old, the three of us—Charlie, Richard, and I—were coming down the road on the bicycle. It had recently rained, and the bicycle wheels slipped. I went one way, Charlie went one way, and Richard flew the other way. I was laid out on the road, unconscious. Charlie and Richard later told me that they were very concerned for me and frightened. Charlie had said, "Oh God! I hope he's not dead because Mom's going to kill us!" When they picked me up, Charlie said it was the greatest thing to know that I was not seriously injured. I believe I had the breath knocked out of me. Charlie slapped me and said, "You all right? You okay?" Then they grabbed me under my arms and walked me around. I was still in a daze, but I was okay. Thankfully, we were never seriously injured. However, those are special memories of my brothers and that bike.

Pigs for Sale!

I will never forget the first time (around age six) I watched in horror as my father cut a hog's throat. It frightened me so much that I can still remember each minute in that moment. Sometimes, my father would kill my favorite hog or piglet that I loved. Dad would put a sign on Moreland Avenue that said, "Pigs for Sale," and people would come by, both black and white, and buy pigs for $15 or $20 apiece. My brothers Richard and Charlie would catch the piglets for the buyer. When I was about eleven years old, I would get into the pen and help catch the pig the buyer wanted. We would then put the pig in a croaker bag (sack) to get it out of the pen. Dad would use the money from the sale of the pig to purchase school supplies, groceries, and clothing.

I do not remember having beef. We had a lot of pork because of the hogs—pork chops, and plenty of pork sausage. Mom made her own lye soap from the leftover parts after the hogs were killed. She would boil the fatty parts of the pork in a big, black pot outside in the yard to make soap. I later learned this was a chemical process called saponification. To make it smell a little better, Mom would add a little perfume to the mixture. Our skin always had the faint residue smell of Mom's homemade soap.

CHAPTER 5
THE JOY OF LIVING

Moving to Turner Way

There have been valleys in my life and yet the mountain tops have been magnificent. I have beautiful memories of great moments in my life.

When I was around twelve years old, my father moved the family to the third home at 961 Turner Way in the Thomasville neighborhood. I loved this house, because we had our first indoor bathroom. With indoor plumbing I did not have to draw water from the well and carry it to the house, and we did not have to use the outhouse for the bathroom; best of all, no more washing chamber pots (portable pots that were used as household toilets). Not only that, we had gas in the house for cooking and electric lights and did not have to use wood anymore. Some of my older siblings—Nathaniel, George, Robert, Ruth, and Viola—had moved out and joined the Army, gotten married, and so on. Therefore, we had a little more room in the house for those of us still living there.

My father owned a Ford Model T. He had it when he was employed during WWII at the Bell Bomber Plant. Mom would prepare him a brown sack lunch, and whatever he could not eat, he would bring home. When Dad got home from work, we would all run up to greet him. Dad would then pass out the cold leftover sausage biscuits. They were the best-tasting biscuits in the world! Sometimes, when it is warm out, I get a whiff of what smells like those sausages and I cannot help but smile at the memory.

The Secrecy of it All

When I was about twelve or thirteen years old, Charlie, Richard, and I had other fun times hanging out together. We had a lot of secrets and hiding spots. We would hide in the woods in little houses we made from straw. Because we lived near the woods, people would dump stuff like broken toys and boxes of household items that were not sellable. We would sift through all of the junk and find some nice things that we would take home. Once we found books that someone had dumped there. Mom made us throw half of them away, especially those that had pictures of naked girls, and we knew Mom would not let us keep them so we hid them from her. The secrecy of it all was fun as well.

My World of Music

My mother was an exciting woman, and she inspired each of us to prepare ourselves for life. She knew that I loved music. When I was thirteen years old, Mom signed me up for a trumpet class and made sure I received a trumpet. It cost $59.95 at Sears Roebuck Department Store. My sister Thelma wanted to play the trumpet too. Everything I did, Thelma wanted to do. Mom bought two trumpets. They cost a total of $118. This was in 1952. That was a lot of money, with a five-dollar-a-month payment plan. I worked as a paperboy, cut grass, and worked in a grocery store to help Mom with the payments.

Mom allowed and made provisions for me to enjoy my kind of music, not blues or rock 'n' roll, but classical music. She paid for mail-ordered music lesson from The U.S. School of Music so I could spend my money on other things. She bought me classical record albums with the speed of 33 1/3 RPMs. I wanted to listen to classical music because it was relaxing. When my brothers and sisters wanted me to listen to other music, such as blues or jazz, Mom would say, "Leave Frazier alone."

Playing the Trumpet

In the eighth grade, I was learning to play the trumpet. Mr. Kenneth Days was my bandleader. My love for music continued to increase. By the time I reached high school, I was part of the advance band and enjoyed being able to wear the band uniform.

In high school, I met an exciting bandleader, Dr. Alfred Wyatt. Dr. Wyatt taught me the importance of music and how it brings out the best in all areas of education. Because of his influence, I was able to play my trumpet as guest soloist at the Atlanta Symphony Orchestra – Haydn's Trumpet Solo, under the direction of Dr. Henry Sopkins. I was an honor roll student when I was sixteen. I loved music; I played the trumpet and a little piano. I became the first trumpet soloist for Luther Judson Price High School band under the direction of Dr. Alfred Wyatt.

At the age of eighteen, I was given the opportunity to play a trumpet solo with the Atlanta Symphony Orchestra under the direction of Dr. Henry Sopkins. I was honored to play Haydn's Trumpet Concerto, First Movement.

As I recall, I was very nervous but also excited. Dr. Wyatt gave me the confidence I needed with these words: "Frazier, you are the only person who knows that song, so play it with all of your heart."

I remember missing just one note, but it was not noticeable unless you had a full knowledge of the selection. The introduction to the music before my solo was about forty-five seconds long. The girl I was dating, Nancy (my future wife) later stated that she thought I had forgotten the music. I later explained to Nancy, I was waiting for the appropriate time to come in. The introduction was very long.

Playing the Piano

When I was in my early teens, about fourteen years old, I was one of the musicians at our church, Mount Carmel AME. I played the piano in the youth choir. Because I already played the trumpet, I could read music, and taught myself to play the piano. My aunt Martha Maddox gave us an old organ when she died. I learned how to work, lead, and teach vocal singing to the youth choir. That was a learning curve for me. My best friend, Willie Franklin Carmichael Jr., also played the piano.

VOLUME 29

Price Student To Play With The Atlanta Symphony

FRAZIER B. TODD

Frazier B. Todd, son of Mr. and Mrs. Floyd Todd, senior of Price High and first chair trumpeter of the Price High Band, will be guest soloist of the Atlanta Symphony Orchestra Concert for the Atlanta Public Schools at the Municipal Auditorium, on March 15th, at 12:30 p. m.

After expressing a desire in 1955 to be the student guest soloist, Todd worked diligently under the supervision of his band director, A. D. Wyatt, to the realization of his dream. He made his debut as a soloist on the 1957 spring concert of the band and chorus. The same year, Todd received the very first award given by the school band to the best all around musician.

The talented musician is very active in church, civic, and school affairs. He is a member of the Mt. Carmel A. M. E. Church, vice president of the school band, president of the Science Club and member of the Honor Society, the Student Council and other organiza-

IGH TIMES

Support The Staff

gh School — Atlanta, Georgia — Price Ten Cents

rice Students epresented At Y-Teen World Fellowship onference

By M. V. EZZARD

wo of Price High School's Y-ens were selected to represent e school at the Y-Teen World llowship Conference which nvened in New York City and ashington, D. C. They were renda Jefferson, a junior, and yrtle Ezzard, a senior.

The conference was held from vember 10-18. During the nference week, many interest- g and educational sights were en.

The purpose of the conference as to acquaint Y-Teens of all ationalities with the objectives the Y-Teens.

The conference proved to be ucational, enjoyable and profit- le.

ience Club Attends avalcade of Medicine

By W. F. CARMICHAEL

The members of the Science ub and advisers were among multitude of students and izens who attended the Cobb ounty Cavalcade of Medicine at arietta, Georgia on November 1956.

The purpose of the exhibition

(Continued on Page Three)

usic Department In mas Carol Concert

By GERALDINE COOK

The music department of Price igh presented the band and al groups in a program of ristmas music on Sunday eve- ng, December 16, at 3:30 p. m. The over capacity audience emed to have appreciated the ur long artistic performance hich included selections from ferent lands as well as dif- t talent and training were

FRAZIER TODD

Frazier Todd, Guest Artist at Symphony Concert

Frazier Todd, Price High senior, will be guest soloist of the Atlanta Symphony Orchestra Concert at the Municipal Auditorium on March 15th, at 12 o'clock noon.

The very talented trumpeter was auditioned by Henry Sopkin, director of the Atlanta Symphony Orchestra. He played as his audition number "Hy Cintho."

Frazier made his debut in the

(Continued on Page Six)

Dr. Sanders Addresses English Department

By MADELYN KING

Dr. Helen Sanders, chairman of the English Department at Spelman College, spoke to the members of the English Department at Price High School on December 10.

Dr. Sanders spoke to the group concerning the requirements of freshman students in college. She also mentioned some of the weak points of students. Dr. Sanders left with them some helpful points on preparing students for college. At the conclusion of the address

Atlanta Daily World- local newspaper article announcing Frazier Todd Sr.'s debut performance Atlanta Symphony Orchestra, Atlanta, GA 1957.

GUEST SOLOIST — Atlanta Symphony Orchestra Conductor, Henry Sopkin, discusses opportunities of the future with Frazier B. Todd, Price High senior. The young trumpeter was guest soloists Friday at the Young Peoples Concert. His rendition was the first movement of Haydns Trumpet Concerto. — (Perry's Photo)

Atlanta Symphony Orchestra conductor (1958) introducing young Frazier B. Todd Sr., age 18 to the Young Peoples Concert.

Frazier B. Todd Sr., 1957, Atlanta, GA

CHAPTER 6
THE PRE-TEEN YEARS

The Atlanta Public School

After I graduated from elementary school in the seventh grade, the City of Atlanta school officials assigned me to attend middle school at David T. Howard High School for the eighth and ninth grades. Later, I was assigned to Luther J. Price High school for the tenth, eleventh, and twelfth grades. My family home was located in unincorporated Atlanta, specifically Fulton County. Fulton County paid the City of Atlanta to educate all black students to the high school level. The school system was segregated during this time until integration in Atlanta, which happened in the late sixties and early seventies.

Money in the Bank

One of my fondest memories as a preteen is of my best childhood friend, Willie Franklin Carmichael Jr. when we were younger. His father worked at General Motors, located in southeast Atlanta. Willie and I had heard that people put their money in the bank. We wanted money, so one day Willie and I tried to get some money out of the "bank," which we pretended was on the hill. We would dig holes in the hill looking for the money that people put in the "bank." My mother would get annoyed because I always showed up to the house dirty.

Willie and I are still friends. Willie received his bachelor's degree from Morris Brown College and received his master's degree from Atlanta University. He retired as a professor of biology from the City of Atlanta Public School System.

At the age of fourteen, I had a paper route with the *Atlanta Constitution* morning newspaper. I would deliver the papers in the morning. My brother Richard had the evening route with the *Atlanta Journal* newspaper.

Cooking and Washing

Growing up, we all had specific chores that Mom assigned us. When I was fourteen years old, my responsibilities were to help take care of the cooking and washing dishes. Mom taught me how to cook barbeque ribs, cornbread, baked beans, macaroni and cheese, peach cobbler, and other dishes. My siblings and I all had to learn how to wash our own clothing. My family did not have a washing machine. I learned how to use a washboard to clean my clothes and then hang the clothes on an outside line with clothes pens. I took Home Economics in high school so I could learn how to do things, such as sew my own clothes when they needed repair.

New Age of Entertainment

After the Korean War ended in 1953, there was a new age of entertainment. The television was black-and-white. My favorite newspaper comics were The Lone Ranger and Dick

Tracey. Dick Tracey had a clock radio on his wrist that he could use to call anywhere in the world. That was so unique.

The children of today have so much liberty with technology. With smartphones and the internet, people can reach out and see the whole world in an instant. My siblings and I had to see the world two or three days later through the news media. We would hear about something and could not see it. The television was groundbreaking, even if only in black and white. When I was in the tenth grade, we got our first television. It was a twelve-inch screen, black-and-white. To make it color, we put a little clear chrome color film over it and it looked just like a color television. Now, with social media, you can receive information before it is even broadcast on the news.

CHAPTER 7
A BLACK BOY IN THE DEEP SOUTH

Picking Cotton

I grew up in a time of segregation, with Jim Crow laws. Jim Crow laws were laws that separated whites from blacks, such as white bathrooms and black bathrooms, or blacks sitting at the back of the bus and whites sitting at the front.

I remember hearing Mom and Dad talk about picking cotton when I was thirteen. Both my parents grew up in the South and picked cotton when they were younger. As a result, I wanted to learn how to pick cotton.

There was a person named Jack Hurd, a black man who came into our neighborhood every summer and gave some of us in the community jobs. He would take people to his small farm about ten miles away. He had several acres of land and a plantation. He would take us out to pick cotton.

One day, I said, "Mom, I want to go pick cotton."

She frowned and pursed her lips. "No, you wouldn't want to do that."

I said, "Mom, please let me go." Therefore, she allowed me to go.

I was around thirteen years old when Mr. Hurd gave me my bag to pick cotton. I was excited at the time. I always loved the way the cotton fields looked, how the landscape would be filled as far as the eye could see with white, fluffy bulbs. However, every time I reached up to pick cotton, I would hurt my hand on one of those cotton bulbs. I thought, oh my God, this is too treacherous! I did not want to continue hurting my hand!

After a half-hour, when I had maybe ten pieces of cotton in the bag, I told Mr. Hurd, "I don't think I want to work here."

Mr. Hurd smiled and said, "That's all right. Your mom already told me to bring you back home."

After that, it occurred to me that my parents certainly knew my temperament. Mom knew I was not going to do anything to mess up my hands. First, I always had clean hands. No matter what everyone else was doing, my hands were always clean, pretty, and soft. I went back home and Mom just smiled and chuckled.

Emergency Room for Colored People

I became interested in girls when I reached high school. One day I was skating with some other youths on the only paved street we had in our community. I was showing off for a girl, Nancy L. Martin. I had just learned how to roller skate. I put my skates on and was doing the Charlie Chan—skating backward and crossing my legs one over the other. The girl I had a crush on must have been impressed because four years later, Nancy became my first wife and the mother of my first three children.

That day, however, my neighborhood friend Jimmy Harvey and I were skating in the road when Jimmy Harvey crashed into me accidentally, throwing me into the pathway of another skater. I went one way and the other skater went the other, and I fell and broke my leg. I do not remember much after that except that my sister-in-law LaVernia who was pregnant at the time (Nathaniel's wife) ran over to me and picked me up off the street. LaVernia lived in the corner house and she sat me down on her porch. I was in severe pain. My leg was on fire, and I had no idea what had happened. We did not have a car at that time, and my older brothers were living away from home, so Mom flagged down a man and he took me to Atlanta's Grady Memorial Hospital. It was a Saturday, and I will never forget that day. I waited in the colored emergency room until the doctor was able to see me.

The doctor sent me to get an X-ray. The X-ray technician was a white woman who treated me terribly. She just threw me onto the table without any regard to the pain I was experiencing. I did not want to cry. At that time, the hospital staff was all white. We had entered the hospital at the colored entrance. I later learned that there was also a white entrance.

The orthopedic specialist looked at the X-ray and told my mom, "The big bone in your son's leg is broken." He would have to set my tibia bone and put a long cast up to my hip. He then grabbed my leg and just popped it hard. I screamed because it was so painful. Then he put on this long cast all the way up to and around my hip. My knee was bent, and I had to learn how to walk with crutches. I was sent back to the X-ray technician, the mean white woman, and she threw me back onto the table and took another X-ray. I had to go back to the doctor so he could see if the fracture was properly set. Even now, all these years later, I have residual discomfort from my injury, especially when it rains.

Segregated Beach

At the age of fourteen, I took my very first trip to the old segregated beach, American Beach, in Florida. My mother gave me permission to take my very first Greyhound bus trip with the Junior Elks. The Junior Elks club were founded on principles of equality. This was a very exciting time for me. One of my best friends, the late Robert Johnson, and his mother, were members of the local Elks Club of Atlanta. I saw for the very first time the Atlantic Ocean. I walked, played, and even built a sandcastle tower on the beach. The sand was so beautiful, and watching the waves come in gave me a thrill I had never experienced before. I realized later in my adult life this was the seed that was planted to give me the ambition to travel throughout the world without fear.

Racial Tension

As a young black male from the Deep South, we were taught at an early age not to play with or tease white girls. I knew the consequences could be serious, so I tried to have as few interactions with them as possible. That was also difficult.

I lived in a community where it was virtually impossible to avoid white people. At the grocery store where I worked, Pill's Grocery Store, the butcher, who was white, lived in an attached dwelling in the back of the store. He had a daughter around my age. Sometimes she would hide in the warehouse. When I would go out into the warehouse to retrieve some boxes to restock the grocery shelves, she would jump out from behind the boxes and scare me. Oftentimes she would place her hands over my eyes and shout, "Guess who?" Without a doubt, she knew that I knew who she was. She would not move her hands from my eyes until I turned around, and then she would steal a kiss on my lips. I would make every excuse not to go into the warehouse without an adult.

Mrs. Ida (a white woman), who was part storeowner of Pill's Grocery store, realized something was going on, so she later would accompany me to the storage room for additional stocks. Mrs. Ida's presence was probably a deterrent to a situation that would have been dangerous if someone had seen the white daughter kissing me.

Late one summer, I was asked to deliver groceries via bicycle to another customer. She was an attractive, middle-aged white woman. Upon entering her apartment with the groceries, I was startled to see her answer the door wearing only her panties. The normal procedure was to place the groceries from the delivery basket at the door. The recipient would then take the groceries, pay or sign the ticket, and you would be on your way back to the store to pick up another set of deliveries. However, I was startled even more when she asked me to place the drinks in the fridge, take out each box, and place them into her cabinets. The entire time I was working she stood so close our bodies touched, wearing a big grin on her face. I was more than shocked.

I gathered my composure and remained respectful under these circumstances. I finished up and departed quickly. Upon returning to the store, I ran and told Mrs. Ida that I did not want to deliver groceries to that woman's home again. Apparently, she understood. From that day on, she made all the deliveries to that apartment. Mrs. Ida was my guardian angel in each of these situations.

Mark of a Real Black Man

I enjoyed the freedom of travel. The feeling of being on the open road further amplified my desire to get my driver's license. I have always had the utmost respect for my dad, but he became my hero when I was a teenager. I was sixteen and wanted to get my driver's license. Most of my friends had their licenses, so I asked a few friends to go with me to the driver's license bureau, known by many as the Department of Motor Vehicles (DMV).

When I arrived at the DMV, I encountered a white man who was taking applications for the license. The man asked me my age and I told him I was sixteen. He raised his eyebrows and said, "Do you have a birth certificate?" I did not have my birth certificate, so he insisted I go home and come back with one of my parents.

Disappointed but not discouraged, I went home and told my dad that he needed to go to the DMV with me because the white man there was not going to serve me because he apparently did not believe that I was sixteen years old. My father accompanied me as I requested. When we arrived at the DMV, the white man said to my dad, "Uncle, how old is your boy?"

Dad arched his brow and said, "I don't think you and I are related." Then he asked, "How old did he say he was?"

The white man replied, "Sixteen."

Then my dad boldly said, "Then that's how old he is."

I saw my dad demand respect for us, with no fear. This incident revealed to me a mark of a real man. My dad emboldened me as only a father could.

My Rage

However, it all came to a head in 1955. When I was about sixteen, my sister Thelma and I had a side business, Todd Cleaning Service. We cleaned new homes, inside and outside, in developments all over Atlanta, including Decatur and southwest Atlanta. We used hydrochloric acid to clean the bricks on the outside. Wherever new homes were being built, we were there to outbid the other companies.

One day, the car broke down. A white man approached Thelma, who was a beautiful eighteen-year-old, and put his hand on Thelma's face, almost touching her nose, and said, "You are a cute little girl."

Enraged, I gritted my teeth and said, "Take your goddamn hand off my sister's face. If you touch her, I'll kill you!" I told Thelma to get back into the car and lock the door.

Then I ran about a mile home to get my dad's twelve-gauge shotgun. I was blinded with rage. My mom saw me leaving the house with the shotgun and shouted, "Boy, what's wrong with you?" Mom tackled me on the front porch and grabbed the shotgun. I explain to Mom the urgency of the situation. Several of my siblings overheard this and ran back to the car, and I followed.

Thelma was still sitting in the front seat with the doors locked and the white man was nowhere to be seen. My brother Ernest had brought his car and was able to jump-start the battery in the car and then we all drove home.

That was a turning point in my life because it allowed me to recognize my anger at the disrespect my sister and I received from this white man.

Emmitt Till's Murder Affected My Life

My rage was a direct result of the news of Emmitt Till's murder. Emmitt was a fourteen-year-old black boy who was murdered for allegedly flirting with a white woman, Carolyn Bryant, in 1955. Bryant's husband and brother-in-law kidnapped Emmitt tortured and murdered him, solely because he was black. The news story of Emmitt Till's murder affected my life. We were of the same age and black, living in the South. I was finally able to understand the reality of racism in America. It made me angry. The injustice of it all enraged me. I knew then that I always had to be careful, because if there had been an assumption I had made an advance to a white girl, I may have been killed like Emmitt Till.

I lived in a time when blacks and whites were segregated, a tumultuous time when the Jim Crow laws mandated what blacks could and could not do; where we could go, or even where we could sit. However, that was all beginning to change. In 1954, Brown versus the Board of Education (Topeka, Kansas) made it to the Supreme Court. The Court stated laws establishing separate educations for whites and blacks to be unconstitutional in a landmark case. In 1955, Rosa Parks, a black seamstress in Montgomery, Alabama, would become an icon as she refused to give up her seat on the bus to a white person. Things were changing.

* * *

The Family's Last Move

In 1955, Dad moved the family to a bigger house on Forest Park Road in Thomasville, a paved road. The address was 1810 Forest Park Road. I was around fourteen at the time and a freshman in high school. My family had electricity, gas, indoor plumbing, and an indoor bathroom. It was a beautiful, white-painted home. There was one bathroom in the house. The girls would go into the bathroom, fix their hair and spend a lot of time in there. The girls had whatever the styles were back in the day. The funny thing about the girls was their hair. They all had a straightening comb. The boys had to run to try to get into the bathroom first, so Mom made some bathroom rules: the boys went first and the girls would go last, and then we would debate between ourselves. At least two of the girls could get into the bathroom at the same time, but the boys and girls could not go in there together, so we had a unique system. We worked it out so everyone could get in and out in a timely manner. That was my last real address with my parents.

It was my address while I attended college and before I went into active duty in the military in the US Army. Years later, my father passed away when we lived at this house. It was the last home he provided for the family while he was alive.

CHAPTER 8
FAMILY FOUNDATION

Floyd Henry Todd

My father, Floyd Henry Todd, was born around 1885 and grew up in Green County, Georgia. He married his first wife, Idona Jackson, in Eaton, Georgia on January 29, 1904. They had seven children: Henry, Betsy, Melvina (Viney), Elease, Eddie, George, and Jimmie. According to the 1920 census, all of my brothers and sisters of my father and Idona were mulatto, as Idona's father was a white man. Idona died of childbirth complications.

My father's second wife was Ola Lee Holt of Forsyth, Georgia (near Macon). Their marriage was recorded in Crawford County, Georgia on November 2, 1923. From this union came one boy and two girls—Robert, Ruth, and Viola Francis. At the time of this writing, all the children from my father's first two wives are deceased, except for Viola. Viola, who was born in 1930, is my oldest living sister. After Ola and my father moved to a new house, Ola became sick and died six months after giving birth to Viola.

My father was a compelling man with a small frame, and powerful presence. He was about 5' 4" and weighed about 140 pounds. He was my hero growing up. He continued to work for the government at the plant, which is now Lockheed Aircraft Industry. Later he worked for the Atlanta General Army Depot, which was located in Conley, Georgia. The depot was later named Fort Gilliam.

Floyd Henry Todd was an interesting man. He was an innovator and a motivator. He was a father, a husband, and a brother to two sisters that I know of, Martha and Ola Todd. He loved farming, and taught farming techniques to the family. He used our two acres of land at Phillips Dr. to produce multiple crops such as corn, sweet potatoes, okra, tomatoes, and beans.

My father was an active member of the community, the Parent Teacher Association (PTA) at Thomasville Elementary School, and in the church setting. He was an officer of Mount Carmel AME Church. He was a steward and a class leader. My father was an active reader of the Bible and other books. He wanted a good education for each of his children. His family was important to him. His talents were praying, organizing, and hunting. He was very knowledgeable about the weather. He knew what temperature and time of year was good to plant crops.

Floyd Todd was also generous, and gave to those in need. When we lived on Phillips Drive, our house was not too far from the railroad (near Forest Park Road and Norwood Manor). When word got out that hitchhikers from the train were in the neighborhood, no matter what color they were, they would often stop by our house and Dad would allow them to sleep on the front porch and feed them.

My Dad loved the Lord. He loved to take part in all the church affairs. Every night before bedtime was family prayer. The manifestation of our family's grace was a result of my father, who understood the necessity of walking this life with Jesus as his navigator.

Mary Alice Smith Todd

My mother, Mary Alice Smith Todd, was a beautiful woman who grew up in Musella in Crawford County, Georgia. She was the youngest girl in her family. She was introduced to motherhood by way of birthing my older brother, Nathaniel Smith. His father is from a previous relationship, before she married my father.

The story of how my parents got engaged is very memorable because they were an unlikely twosome and had a long and fruitful marriage. She lived next door to my father. According to Mom, her father, Charlie Smith, and my father, were friends.

One day, my father told Charlie, "I need a wife."

Charlie said, "Well, my daughter Mary Alice is young, about seventeen or eighteen, and she has a baby."

My father said, "That will do."

Charlie called my mom over and said, "Floyd wants to marry you."

Mom replied, "If that's what you want, I'll do it." That is how my parents got together. My father's first and second wives died and left him a widower with children to raise. My mother was not much older than some of my siblings my father had with Idona and Ola. My mom had a big heart and was willing to take on the responsibility of raising some of my father's children. My parents came to love each other, and they were happily married over 50 years. It always amazed me how my parents came together. If I could have a conversation with my mother today, I would ask her about her mother and father. I would love to know what my maternal grandfather, Charlie and my maternal grandmother, Carrie Blasingame were like.

Mary Alice was a devoted mother. She had sparkling brown eyes, long black hair, and she had a beautiful smile. When I was young, Mom was always cooking and preparing food on the wood-burning stove in the kitchen. My mother made sure we always had breakfast before we went to school and everybody had clean clothes. She made certain that the children were a positive reflection of her in our community.

One of the proudest things I remember was the smile on her face when we would do something exciting. She would just beam and say we were the smartest kids in the world. She insisted that we study our lessons and have respect for our elders. I am eternally grateful that my mother instilled good manners and a respectful attitude in all of us. Mom showed no favoritism among her children; we all were equal and important in her life. Although I knew I was her favorite, she made us all feel that each of us was special and the favorite one. That was the great beauty of her life.

Mary Alice was an amazing mother of the church. She believed in Jesus, our Lord and Savior; in God, our Father; and in the Holy Spirit, our Comforter. She believed that with all of her heart. She took us to church at Mount Carmel AME, including to Sunday school and evening services. She always dressed in white on Communion Sunday.

My mother and father were unique parents. They raised us in such a loving and creative way that as a child, I did not realize I was poor. They took care of all of us and did not have much materially.

My Siblings

I had a wonderful relationship with my siblings from childhood to adulthood. I did not have an opportunity to meet my siblings Henry Lee, Betsy Ann, or Jimmie, because they were so much older and had either moved out of the house or were deceased by the time I was born.

My sister Thelma loved to play basketball. She played on the team at Turner High School in Atlanta. She graduated from college and served as associate pastor at the Church of Hope Ministries (COHM).

My brother Charlie inspired me. Charlie retired as a mechanical engineer. He was the first one in the family to graduate from college. He was not the first one to go to college. He and my brother Ernest were college classmates.

My brother Larry managed a hair-product company, he was a successful relator in metro Atlanta, and he served as a Sr. Deacon in the church.

My brother Richard, who was four years older than I was, moved to Michigan to work at General Motors at an early age. He served in the US Marine Corps before the Vietnam era.

My brother Lee Ernest moved to Michigan when he was a young adult to get a job for the summer. He only stayed for two months. His lifelong career was working for Atlanta Life Insurance Company.

My sister, Melvina, was a businessperson and owned a nightclub with her husband on Coney Island in New York in the mid-1960s.

My sister Elease lived in Atlanta, and her husband worked for the railroad. My sister Thelma lived with Elease during the summer.

My sister Eddie lived in Brooklyn, New York, and visited Atlanta regularly, especially during the Christmas holidays.

My sister, Ruth, was remarkably close to me.

After I broke my leg when I was fourteen, I stayed with Ruth to recuperate for about three months.

My sister Viola Francis is a very studious woman. She always looked after me in elementary school and called me her "little brother." She and her daughters, Rosa, Jeannette, and son, Willie are members of (COHM) where I am the senior pastor.

My sister, Mattie Jean, was an exciting and intelligent woman. She worked extremely hard in school. She was a committed woman of the gospel and worked as one of my nurses in my medical practice. She had a heavenly singing voice.

My sister Carolyn is the youngest of all my siblings. She is a college graduate and a dynamic and outspoken woman. I often called her a "mama's baby girl." She works diligently in the church and the community. She also worked as a medical transcriptionist in my medical practice.

My brother, Robert, was an extraordinarily talented singer. He lived in New York. The quartet group that he was a member of once performed at Carnegie Hall in New York.

My big brother George lived in New York. He was a real family-oriented person who took extremely great care of his family and was a devoted husband.

My brother Willie James was buried one day after his birth in 1945.

My brother Nathaniel was the oldest of my mom's children. He was a minister, pastor, and leader and dedicated to the Lord, and his work and family. He was one of the first (while I was the overseer pastor) to conduct revival at Davis Chapel AME Church in Forest Park, Georgia. When he was honorably discharged from the United States Army, he returned home to Atlanta and married LaVernia. They had several children together.

Family Traditions

Our family traditions were centered on church activities which included dinners and sharing of food. Sunday traditions included breakfast (before church) of grits with mackerel fish. Mom would add two or three cups of flour to the mackerel to stretch it. In the hog-killing season, we would have pork chops. We would also have biscuits. The Sunday traditional dinner meal would be chicken, cornbread, and collard greens or black-eye peas. It was our family tradition every Sunday.

On Saturdays, a family member would go to the yard, kill four to five chickens, and prepare them for the meal on Sunday. The family had hundreds of chickens at one time. My brother Ernest was one of the better cooks. He would pluck the chickens, and help prep the chickens for Mom to cook on Sunday. Once a year, we would have a big church outing we called the Family Reunion. Later, when we were older, we would go to an annual celebration at Mom's home church in Crawford County in Musella, Georgia for the homecoming celebration.

There are many ministers in my immediate family. One of our family traditions was to develop ministers so we would all understand our purpose of sharing the good news of the gospel. For example, my parents would encourage my siblings and me to attend Sunday school, the morning, evening, and night service. There was home Bible study and family prayer time. We would take part in all holiday's plays that included Christian characters.

Holidays with the Family

As a young black boy growing up in the South, holidays were special. The big holidays were Christmas and Easter. They were good times because they centered on church activities. We had plays and skits at the church, along with the hiding of eggs, either at church, at home, or wherever we were. It was fun! Even though we moved three times, we always lived in the Thomasville community. We celebrated Easter with Easter eggs and Christmas with letters to Santa Claus and the sharing of gifts. Santa Claus always came, and my parents always bought every child one item.

We celebrated all our holidays in big style. We always had a Christmas tree on Christmas; we would pick out a tree in the woods and chop it down. We would get the best-looking one and we would make a stand for it out of plain wood and nails. If it was leaning a little bit, we would box it up, so it was straight. We made our own homemade decorations with colored paper and glue. We even made our own star at the top. With a large family, we did not have the extra money to go out and buy ornaments.

Mom and Dad would say, "Christmas is around the corner." As children, we could not wait for Christmas to come, so we would run up to the corner of our road looking for Christmas to come around the corner!

On New Year's Eve, we all went to church. The Fourth of July was another day for us to play. On Memorial Day weekends, we honored the soldiers because I had brothers who were veterans of war.

My Grandchildren

My father worked hard. Just as he was proud of us, I am proud of him. I am proud of my off springs who I am passing family traditions to. The best thing for me being a parent, a grandparent, and a great-grandparent, is observing my children grow up.

All my grandchildren and great-grandchildren are dynamite! I love them because they are magnificent. I love the quote "Grandchildren should have come first (before the children)". My grands are: Denaya, Levonne, Cynthia, Jennifer, Ronald, Frazier Ben III, Niah, Tamia, Ory, Kai, Akio, Kobi, Jaylin, Dayana, Dylan, Isaiah, Genesis, Jordan Phillip, Jordan Josiah, Jordan, Jasper IV and Skyler.

STATE OF GEORGIA

COUNTY OF Clayton

STATE OF GEORGIA 1776

To Floyd ~~Collins~~ Todd Esq., Greeting:

IN ACCORDANCE WITH THE LAWS OF THIS STATE, and in pursuance of your election by the voters of your School [Di]strict and of the action of the County Board of Education of said County, the County Board of Education does hereby [co]mmission you a Trustee of Riverdale Col School ~~District~~ for the term ending Jan 1 1943

SEAL

Date 1/9/40

YOU ARE, therefore, hereby authorized and required to perform all the duties incumbent on you as a Trustee aforesaid according to law and the trust reposed in you. This commission is to continue in force during the active and efficient service and for the term pointed out by the laws of the State, which say that this certificate shall be your sufficient warrant for entering upon and performing the duties of your office. These duties are as follows: To visit the schools as often as practicable; to inspect the school work done; to make recommendations to the Board of Education for the advancement of the school interests; to aid, by recommendation of desirable applicants, the County Superintendent and Board of Education in securing teachers; in keeping the school house and grounds in good condition and equipped for good work; to aid the county educational authorities in keeping the school supplied with fuel, water, and proper sanitary necessities; to make a written report once a year and oftener, if necessary, to the County Board of Education.

As you have the opportunity, impress upon patrons and pupils the importance of regular attendance, of hearty home cooperation, and of establishing and using school libraries.

Given under my hand and seal of the County Board of Education, the 9th day of January in the year of our Lord, One Thousand Nine Hundred and Forty

[A]TTEST: [signature] President Board of Education.

W. L. Gilbert County Superintendent of Schools.

Frazier Sr., father, Floyd Todd, certificate of a Trustee for the local school board in 1943, Riverdale, GA.

Frazier Sr., mother, Mary Smith Todd and sister, Joan at the house on Baker Rd, Atlanta, GA.

Frazier Sr.'s sister, Mattie Jean Todd approximately twenty four years old.

Frazier Sr., and brother, Lee Ernest.

Charlie Todd

Frazier Sr.', brother, young Charlie Todd

Frazier Sr.'s sisters. Left to right: Ruth, Viola, Thelma and Joan Todd at church early 2000's

Frazier Sr.'s youngest sister
Carolyn Todd, Atlanta, GA

Frazier Sr.'s, sister: Elease Todd.

Frazier Sr.'s brother, George Henry Todd.

Frazier Sr.'s sister, Joan Todd approximately twenty-three years old.

Frazier Sr., and brothers; Left to right: Richard, Charlie, Frazier, Larry Todd and church member, Atlanta, GA. (2013)

CHAPTER 9
DEEPLY ROOTED

My Genealogy DNA

My mother told me that she was a mix of white, African, and Native American. According to my genealogy DNA test, I am 94% African with 24% from Benin/Togo, 19% from Nigeria 13% Ivory Coast/Ghana and the remaining percentage from other regions. The number of family members related to me represented from my genealogy DNA test numbered in the thousands. Through this test, I was personally able to meet and or chat with new cousins I never knew existed, namely Zona Gardner of Texas, and Emma Smith of Kentucky. In a surprised twist, I discovered a 96% genealogy DNA test result that matched a distant cousin (Willie Mack Watley) age ninety eight of Louisiana. This cousin (Willie), is also highly related through genealogy DNA testing to Janice Jerome (the lead person for the Todd-Smith Project). WOW what a shocker. There is an old saying that "We are all connected" I highly believe this!

My Maternal Family

My mother's father, Charles (Charlie) Smith, was born around 1869 in Crawford County, Georgia, and died around

1944 in Crawford County, Georgia. When I first met him, he looked like a white man to me. I now know he was a mulatto, someone with black and white ancestry. My brother Charlie was named after my grandfather. My maternal grandmother, Carrie Blasingame (married to Charlie Smith), was born around 1873 in Crawford County, Georgia. Carrie's father, my maternal great-grandfather, Frederick or Fred Blasingame, was born around 1837. He was married to Georgia Annie Jones, who was born around 1846.

Charlie's father (my maternal great-grandfather) Richard Smith, was a mulatto. Richard was born around 1823 and died around 1865 in Georgia. He was married to my great-grandmother, Lucy McCrary Smith. Lucy was born in either 1817, 1821 or 1824 based on various Federal Census. My mother tells a family story that Lucy was from the country of India.

My aunt Carrie Webb was named after her mother Carrie Blasingame. Carrie Webb was like a grandmother figure to me. She was my mother's older sister. Carrie Webb lived in Forest Park, Georgia. Her adult sons had left home in the mid-1940s during World War II, so she selected me to be her new son in the summertime. I called her Aunt Carrie, and I became her surrogate grandson.

Aunt Carrie and Uncle Albert, her husband would do anything I wanted. If I wanted a sweet potato pie, my aunt would make it. If I wanted chocolate cake, she made it. Aunt Carrie spoiled me. Mom let Aunt Carrie spoil me when I visited her.

My Paternal Family

My paternal grandfather, Cleveland (Cleburn) (Clairborn) Todd, was born around 1820 in Georgia and married my grandmother, Melvina (Viney) Watts on January 7, 1883, in Greene County, Georgia. I have not found information on my paternal great-grandparents (Clairborn's parents).

My great-grandparents (Melvina's parents) were Berry Watts (born around 1820) and Amanda Watts (born around 1814).

My grandfather, Cleveland Todd, is listed in the Georgia returns of qualified voters and reconstruction oath books from 1867–1869. My father, Floyd Todd, is on the register for the militia during World War I.

The 2013 Interview

In 2013, I spoke to Janice Jerome, the researcher for the Todd-Smith family project at the National Archives of Atlanta. The purpose of this interview was to examine the early ancestral records of the Todd-Smith family. Janice informed me about the oldest records found on my father, Floyd Henry Todd, from 1899. The following is an excerpt from our conversation.

Dr. Todd: We are reviewing census records of documentation. According to the 1940 census record, my father earned $320 for that year. There were seven family members living in Riverdale—my parents and my siblings, Lee Ernest, Charlie, Richard, Thelma, and of course me, little Frazier. My sister Joan was two years younger than I was. Before she was born, I would ask my mom where my baby sister was, and my mother would reply, "She's still traveling in your father's heavenly bag."

Janice: According to this 1940 US census record, you were one year old.

Dr. Todd: I was a year old at that time. Charles Smith was my grandfather.

Janice: Charlie R. Smith? Is that with an "R" in his name?

Dr. Todd: Yes.

Janice: I noticed in your parents'1940 census record there is a Nathan —he is four.

Dr. Todd: That is Nathaniel. That is the son my mom had before she married Dad.

Janice: I know your mother's name was Mary Alice Smith. Looking at the 1930 census with your grandfather Charlie R. Smith as head of household, there is a Mary Smith. Is this your great-aunt? She was seventy-five in 1930. Is this the one who was born a slave?

Dr. Todd: Yes, my mother, Mary Alice Smith, and my great-aunt Mary Smith shared the same name.

Janice: Your aunt Mary Smith, born in 1855 on Smith Plantation, was seventy-five years old in 1930. She was your grandfather Charlie Smith's sister. He was sixty-one in 1930.

Dr. Todd: Mary Smith was born a slave. That is interesting information. My grandfather was born on the plantation too. He looked like a white man. I wonder what my great aunt Mary Smith looked like.

Janice: This is interesting that Charlie R. Smith was born in 1860. His mother, Lucy, was from Virginia.

Dr. Todd: Yeah. She came from Virginia that is the story my mother told me, she was from the country of India.

Janice: Tell me more about Lucy.

Dr. Todd: She was Lucy Ann, my great-grandmother, and she was married to Richard Smith. Lucy Ann was Charlie R. Smith's mother. Per my mother, she was born in Virginia. Lucy Ann was her slave name. She was from the country of India. She and her sister both slaves were brought to America. They were separated in Virginia.

Janice: Do you know anything more?

Dr. Todd: I do not. Is there an 1890 census?

Janice: The Federal 1890 Census was destroyed in a fire. The first Federal Census was done in 1790 and they are done every ten years. There is a seventy-two-year restriction. I would like you to try to remember certain things. Your father, Floyd Todd, lived in many counties in Georgia. Do you know why he moved around so much? Your father has been recorded as living in Putnam, Greene, Morgan, Monroe, Crawford, Upson, Fulton, Clayton, and Eaton, Georgia.

Dr. Todd: Floyd Todd was a jockey who took part in harness racing. Because of his small stature, he was talented with horses and horseracing.

He traveled throughout the state of Georgia with white and black horse owners. After I read the book *Race Horse Men* by Katherine C. Mooney, I now have a greater appreciation of the subtitle: "How Slavery and Freedom Were Made at the Racetrack." As a child around the age of eight, I heard my father, Floyd, speak of troubles he had with a white man. He said that he had a dispute with a white man. The family he worked for as a jockey hid him and later sent him to another distant county in South Georgia to stay safe. I remember rumors from other older family members that Dad may have killed a white man.

Janice: The earliest information found recorded on Floyd Todd was the 1900 Census of Green County, Georgia, spelled as Floid Tod. He was a servant at the age of fourteen and was born about 1885. He was living with Ann Credille, a white female, along with a boarder and his family. This may be Floyd Todd. This was in Militia District 162–163, Criddelle, Huterson, Greene County, Georgia. The next earliest date I found Floyd Todd was at age twenty-five.

Dr. Todd: That is good to hear.

Janice: He was twenty-five and in Putnam, Georgia, in 1910.

Dr. Todd: If we could find him in 1890—

Janice: The earliest I found him was the 1900 census in Green County, Georgia.

Dr. Todd: I see the names Charlie Smith; he was sixty-one. Mattie B. was twenty-seven, Carrie Smith . . .

Janice: I thought Carrie was your aunt. Are there two different Carries?

Dr. Todd: Carrie is my aunt. She married into the Webb family. She was married to Albert Webb. Carrie was also the name of my maternal grandmother. When you see the census from Crawford County, the Webbs lived next door to the Todds. That is how Charlie Smith and Floyd Todd were friends; they were farmers. After Dad's second wife (Ola) died, Mom [Mary] said that my father needed a woman in the house so he asked Charlie. Charlie said, "Well, I'll call Mary and see." Mary said, "That's what you want, that's what I'll do." My parents never dated, and that is what happened. Carrie was married, so she was not living in the house at that time. She was married to Albert Webb. When I take you to the cemetery, you will see all that history.

Janice: Where is the family cemetery found?

Dr. Todd: There is a family cemetery located in Atlanta off Riverdale Road—Carver Memorial Cemetery. Many of my family members are buried there.

My parents, except for one brother, are buried at Carver Memorial.

Janice: Who is buried in the Smith Cemetery in Musella, Georgia?

Dr. Todd: The Smith Cemetery is where my grandparents on the Smith side of the family are buried. My grandfather's side is all buried in the Smith Cemetery.

Janice: Did you say that your grandfather Charlie was mulatto?

Dr. Todd: Yes, very much so. I thought he was a white man when I saw him as a four- or five-year-old child.

After the interview, I found the research on my family history interesting and refreshing to learn more about my family genealogy.

My brother Charlie who inspired me over the years may know more about my father. I am putting down in writing what I know for the younger generations. I have recorded the family history in this book and published it through the Todd-Smith Family Documents Ancestors-Descendants book (ISBN-13:978-0-9729741-1-0).

The Kufi Cap

Now, let me tell you a side story. Around 1992, I was in Atlanta having lunch near Metropolitan Ave one afternoon (while wearing a kufi on my head). A kufi cap is a brimless, round cap worn in Africa by men in many populations. People in the U.S. with West African heritage wear it to show pride in their culture, history, and religion. It is often made of kente cloth, knitted or crocheted. I wear a cloth kufi hat daily.

That day, a young man from the country of India walked to my table, and he stopped and asked if he could join me for lunch. He was a student in one of the seminaries in Atlanta. He sat down and told me that I resembled one of his uncles from India. I called my mother, she spoke with him, and later, we met very often.

He and his Korean wife, became a member of our congregation. When they finished their seminary training at a Christian school in Atlanta, they left the city of Atlanta, but he told me some interesting things. He said, "You got to be in my family in some kind of way."

He says you can trace your family name in India because they keep excellent records of their heritage. If you find one name, they can go all the way back three or four thousand years to find that information. We did not do any research follow- up on the possibility that we may be related.

Papa Charlie Smith

Frazier Sr.'s maternal grandfather, Charles Smith (Papa) Georgia

Jennie Webb

Frazier Sr.'s first cousin, Jennie Webb

Frazier Sr.'s great aunt and cousin. Left to right: Lillae Mae (Papa Charlie Smith's daughter) and her daughter

Mother: Minnie

Grandpa Charlie Daughter
1 name Sam (Boy)

Frazier Sr.'s distant cousins, Minnie (Papa Charlie's daughter) one son name Sam.

William T Smith
(Little Buddy)

Frazier Sr.'s uncle, both pictures -bottom left to right: William T. Smith and family members (top) Georgia

CHAPTER 10
COMING OF AGE

Luther Judson Price High School

I attended Howard High School for the eighth and ninth grades, and I attended Luther Judson Price High School from the tenth to twelfth grades. Luther Judson Price was a man I admired. He was a local black man who worked as a postal worker and took part in the Atlanta race riot in 1906.

The Atlanta race riot of 1906 was a mass civil disturbance. Prior to the riot, there were continuous conflicts between whites and blacks after the Civil War, and this spilled over into the political arena. The Atlanta newspapers reported that white women had been sexually molested and raped by black men. White men gathered in the streets and beat and stabbed black men in retaliation. Some African-American men were hanged from lampposts. It is my understanding that Luther Judson Price was a peacekeeper and prevailed in the southeast section of Atlanta. Luther Judson Price High School opened its doors in 1954 as the fifth African American high school in Atlanta Public Schools.

High School Classmates and Teachers

Mary Ann Wilson, a high school classmate, attended Howard and Price High School with me, (later became a successful physician in Atlanta), and one my colleagues. I encouraged her to go to medical school. We were the top math students in our class. She and I competed against each other to see who could finish math problems the quickest. Our high school math teacher would put a problem on the board just for us to work on.

My good friend Aaron Jackson and I were champion math students in elementary school. We would go through problems just like that. Even in high school, math was one of my favorite subjects. In 1957 and 1958, I majored in math and chemistry at Morehouse College. I have always excelled in my academic career in mathematics.

My high school algebra teacher, Mr. Allen, taught Mary Ann and me that if we found a math problem we did not recognize we could substitute an equation into the problem and proceed from that point to solve it. When Mary Ann and I entered the classroom, everyone would stare at us, because it was no secret that she and I were competing to be the best math student. If Mary Ann could not solve the problem, I would go in and use Mr. Allen's advice, and it worked! The math teacher was blown away!

Getting Acquainted with Automobiles

When I was sixteen years old, my parents did not have a car. I learned how to drive from a man named Milton Baker Sr., who delivered the morning newspaper, the *Atlanta Constitution*, in my neighborhood. The streets were not paved in my community, and after a heavy rain, it was easy for cars to be stuck in the mud. If we were stuck, Mr. Baker taught me how to sit behind the steering wheel and guide the car while he pushed so we could get out of the mud. I would run up and put the newspaper on the porch while he drove the car. Sometimes I would say, "I hope we get stuck today." I knew if we were stuck, Mr. Baker would have to push the car while I drove the car out of the mud.

"Get him Butler!"

I have always loved cars and sports. However, I almost had a fatal car crash trying to get to a baseball game that I was playing in. My brother Richard and I were members of a baseball team in the Thomasville community. My brother, Richard was the pitcher and I was the batboy. There were five more on the team. One time we were traveling out of town to a game and we were almost killed. My friend Butler was driving an old Delta '88 Oldsmobile. I was in the back seat with four other team members and there were three other team members up front, including my brother Richard.

The Oldsmobile had overdrive. In overdrive, you could pass anything on the road. The highways in those days were just two lanes. Butler was coming up to a black Buick, so we urged Butler on. "Get, him Butler," we said. Butler hit overdrive to go around the car.

Butler was going to pass the Buick, but the Buick driver sped up. Butler was driving for about a half-mile alongside the Buick and the driver would not yield. Butler soon approached a hill when another car, a Ford, was coming over the hill facing us head-on! Boy, Butler did some heroic driving! The other car hit his brakes. Our car, the Oldsmobile, went back and forth across the highway three or four times, this way and that way. Butler was driving eighty to ninety miles per hour!

The Ford did not turn over and crash, and our car, the Oldsmobile, swerved over to the side of the road. We did not crash into the Buick nor the Ford. The Buick continued. We were all shaken up. We were wet, too—I urinated on myself, and someone had thrown up.

Then one car stopped. It was a white man. He said, "You boys were driving dangerously. You could get people killed like that. You better straighten up or I'll call the highway patrol."

We said, "Yes, sir," because we knew we were wrong.

I was sweating. I said, "Mom would kill us all again." I knew it was going to be a lost game when we got there to play ball. My big brother Richard was the starting pitcher. He was knocked out of the game in the first inning. We lost because we were all still shaken up from that event. My clothes were disheveled, wet, and I was frightened.

Being Poor

The most popular thing we had going for us as teenagers was bebop. Bebop is a style of dance started in the 1940s with a fast rhythm. Singers like Billy Einstein, Cab Calloway, and Louis Armstrong were in bands that played bebop music. I was quite good at it. My girl, Nancy, and I loved to dance. We would be the first to get on the floor and the last ones off. Those were some good times. I do not remember any popular movies except for the TV show *Dragnet*, which starred Jack Webb, the detective. I was a Jack Webb fan.

At sixteen, I would attend events at school feeling good about how I was dressed. However, I did not realize we were poor until a classmate said to me in high school, "You guys are poor." He wore the same type of clothes my siblings and I wore.

I replied, "You must be poor too."

We would go to school with mud on our shoes. I lived on a muddy street and I had to walk through the mud to get to the school bus. With the rain and snow, there was always mud. I knew that when I grew up I wanted to be wealthy and secure so I would not have to walk through mud owning one pair of shoes.

Dad Taught the Value of Work

As a teenager Dad would take Richard and I out to cut grass. We put a lawn mower on a streetcar that would take us up to Buckhead in Atlanta. Dad told us to randomly go to the front door of a house and tell a potential customer that if he or she needed their grass cut that we could do it and we charged five dollars. For instance, If I knocked on a door and a lady answered, then I would say "My dad says to ask you if you need your grass cut?"

Then the potential customer would ask, "Where is he?" Right then, my father would wave. The potential customer would say, "Okay, cut the grass." We would cut the grass and she would say, "I have a neighbor down the street. . ." We would go down the street and cut her grass too. Learning how to make honest money was always a joy for me.

When I was seventeen, I made $50 a week in the summer! I made about as much as my father did when he was working full-time at the Bell Bomber Plant during World War II.

I worked at Pill's Grocery Store on McDonough Boulevard across from the Atlanta Federal Penitentiary, and I knew everybody in the community. When the new grocery store (Heap Cheap Grocery) opened in Thomasville they heard from some of the community members that I was a good worker. Because of this, Heap Cheap offered me a job and more money than Pill's. The manager at Heap Cheap said he would pay me $50 a week because he knew I would bring him customers. Although I had a great relationship with the Pills, whose grocery store was across the street from Heap Cheap, I was able to earn more money and make a greater contribution to my family.

I did everything for $50 a week. I was a cashier, clerk, stock boy, delivery person, you name it. The owner of Heap Cheap told me that he would let me use the car to take my girlfriend, Nancy, to the prom in 1957. Of course, I was going to work for him after he offered me a brand-new 1957 Pontiac. Those were great days. By the time, I was ready for college, I had a couple thousand dollars in my savings account. I graduated from Luther Judson Price High School in 1957. I never felt so proud.

MECHANICAL MAN, ROBIE THE ROBOT — Machine's creators, Franklin Lynn and Frazier B. Todd, make him talk and walk. Robot was outstanding feature at Price High Science Fair. — (Perry's Photo)

1956-57 APS School Year The Atlanta World News

Science Fair (Price High School) Frazier Sr., and classmate Franklin Lynn featured in local newspaper (1956-57).

CHAPTER 11
A HEAVY LOSS

"It Broke My Heart"

I was a freshman at Morehouse College when it was time for Dad's transition. It broke my heart. My father, Floyd Henry Todd, died on Sunday, October 20, 1957, because of a cardiovascular episode. Dad was seventy-two years old. I will never forget that Sunday morning when he transitioned very quietly. His funeral (celebration of life) was on Friday, October 25, 1957, in Atlanta at the Mount Carmel AME Church.

Dad had been ill with gangrene after the amputation of his leg secondary to diabetes a few months before. The ambulance came to transport him to the local Grady Memorial Hospital of Atlanta. I was able to ride in the ambulance with him and held his hand. At this time, we did not have emergency 9-1-1 call centers. The emergency transportation was provided by a local funeral hearse method. My brother Lee Ernest had driven his car to the hospital so that I would have a ride back home if Dad was admitted as a patient. Once we arrived at the hospital, my dad was pronounced dead on arrival (DOA). He died holding my hand in the ambulance.

Upon hearing this announcement of DOA, we both were brokenhearted and cried in the emergency room. The hospital did what they could under the circumstances and we left. At that time, my driver's license had been suspended because I had rear-ended a car while driving uninsured.

On the way home from the hospital, my brother was speeding. A police officer pulled us over and was going to give Lee Earnest a speeding ticket, but he spoke up and told the officer that our father had just died and that we wanted to hurry home and deliver the bad news to the family. The officer told Lee Earnest to get out of the car and told me to take over as the driver. When I explained to him my license situation, he wrote a note that stated he was giving me permission to drive until I reported to the Georgia Department of Driver's Service (DDS) to renew my license.

As expected, Mom and the family took the news of Dad's death very hard. Indeed, it was a very difficult time for all of us. I remember walking on the dusty streets that night as tears fell from my eyes to the dirt. Somehow, I ended up at my girl's home on Sharon Avenue in Atlanta. Nancy, her grandmother, and her aunt Hazel were all there, so Nancy comforted me in my time of grief and distress.

The funeral was held the following Friday at the Mount Carmel AME Church. The death of my father was very difficult. Midterms were scheduled at Morehouse that Monday, the day after my father's death. I reported to Dean Brazeal of Morehouse early on that Monday. He sent me home and delayed my midterms until the following week.

Dad's celebration was on the following Friday at the home church. It was beautiful, wonderful, and sad, all in one. I was not able to tolerate the scene as they lowered his casket into the ground. I ran back to the car; Mom came to my rescue and she tried to comfort me as much as possible. The tears flowed from my eyes; however, one thing I drew comfort from was that they buried my father in one of my white shirts.

As I write this, tears burn my eyes as I think of my father, Floyd Henry Todd; my dad, my partner, my hero, and my friend. I now know that when the spirit is absent from the body, it is present with the Lord. My father and my mother both are present with the Lord. One day I will join them and fellowship again with my two best friends in heaven, my mom and dad.

The death of my father was the most difficult challenge of my life. However, it taught me that life is a process, and you learn to adjust to every challenge you face—and there will be many. Through the love, devotion, wisdom, and counseling from my mother, I was able to face this deep loss and still operate without losing my focus on my ultimate goal: to continue my college education.

I passed all of my midterm exams with a B average. It was not easy. I missed my father more than anything. He would have been disappointed if I had not completed my exams with success. I still have my father and mother's picture over the mantle at home. I can see them both each day. I was nineteen, I believed that my parents would live forever; that they would be there for me and see my children grow up. By losing my father, I gained a better appreciation for the standards and character he placed in my life. My father, Floyd Henry Todd, will always be my hero.

CHAPTER 12
MY FIRST LOVE, NANCY

I will never forget Nancy Martin, my first love. I met Nancy Martin in elementary school and had a crush on her. We dated through high school and college. I loved Nancy. She was so beautiful and wise beyond her years. She had been raised by her grandmother and it was evident in her personality. She was frugal with our funds. I was amazed at how she could stretch a dollar. However, she knew how to have a good time. We enjoyed playing cards with our friends, pinochle was our game. And we could dance all night. We were in love with lots of youthful energy and high hopes for our future. I married Nancy in 1958 in Fort Smith, Arkansas. It was a great experience. It felt like my life was falling into place in terms of college, getting married, and starting a family.

While I was away in the military doing basic training, Nancy was attending Spellman College in Atlanta. For the first six months of our marriage we did not have children. This was to our advantage because a military mix-up between the Navy and the Army resulted in me not receiving my pay. The Army paid me ten dollars a month to buy personal toiletries.

Our First Car

After marrying Nancy, we realized that a car was needed for the family. Around December of 1958, I bought my first car while I was in the Army in Aniston, Alabama, from a soldier friend who decided not to re-enlist into the Army. I did not really have the money at the time (Frazier Jr. had just been born). This friend insisted that I needed a car and would sell it to me for $125. The car was in good condition. It had a few rust spots under the door panel from the salt that was put on the road where he lived before his military service in Michigan. It was a four-door 1949 Mercury. I agreed to buy it. We set up a payment plan of $25 down and $25 a month. He signed the title over to me and allowed me to pay him on credit, and I became the new owner. I was blessed again because I needed transportation.

Nancy and I drove home in our new car to Atlanta to spend the holidays and show off our new son to our families. Twenty dollars was all the money I had. We were living by the grace of God because I was not receiving that much ($10 month) payment from the military at that time.

I drove up to the gas station to buy at least $2 worth of gas. Gas was, as I recall, less than twenty-five cents a gallon. It is approximately one hundred miles from Anniston, Alabama, to Atlanta. I had calculated that I would need at least $2 worth of gas to drive that distance. I knew that after we arrived home we would have a place to stay with family, and other accommodations would be available.

When I asked the gas attendant to pump the $2 worth of fuel into the tank, he was only able to pump $1.50 into the tank. I realized the gas gauge was not working properly. However, I did not understand his grace working in my life then, as I understand it today. After we arrived home in Atlanta, the military sent a check for the back pay and other expenses totaling more than $500. Wow! We were rich in December of 1958!

Four years later, in 1962, my family was living in San Antonio, Texas. I was stationed there at Brook Army Medical Center. Nancy and I were house hunting. You could buy a house in Texas for about $15,000 to $20,000 in those days. In San Antonio, you only needed $200 down, with monthly payments of $80 to $90.

At that time, I was promoted to Enlisted 5 (E-5), which is a sergeant. The pay was not bad. I was making $400 a month. Nancy and I had three kids: Frazier Jr., Sandra, and Angela. I could afford to buy a home and pay $80 a month on the house note because it was cheaper than rent.

However, it was a good thing I did not buy a house in Texas in 1962. My best friend, Sergeant Molino, called me up one night and told me that I was going to be transferred overseas to Korea. The move to Korea occurred a few months later.

Nancy and I shared many laughs with our three children. One of the funniest things that happened was when Nancy and I were in Korea with our children. Frazier Ben Todd Jr. was about four years old. Nancy, the children, and I were eating on the military base when Frazier Jr. suddenly jumped up on the table, held up his glass, and started singing, "Do you love me?" A popular song recorded by the Contours for Motown Record Company. I was spellbound because it happened so fast. The people in the restaurant stopped and listened. Frazier Jr. was an entertainer, so I let him sing the song. Many of the soldiers who were present thought it was funny and entertaining.

Nancy and I were married for seven years and we had our challenges. We were married during the years that I was active in the military. Our constant moving, even to foreign countries, South Korea and Japan was very stressful; at times, overwhelming for me and as well as I believe for Nancy. Even though I always took pride in providing for my family (especially spiritually, emotionally, academically and financially), I believe there were times in my absence that Nancy had to be both mother and father to our kids. This includes those days I was on active duty and she alone had to care for the kids when they were sick, help them with their school work and even be there playmate in my absence. I desperately missed my children and Nancy while on active duty. We were separated not by choice, for extended periods of time. I believe it was an enormous strain on both of us. I was very depressed and hurt when our marriage ended in divorce. I immersed myself in my work as a military soldier and took pride in the uniform.

Nancy was a stabilizing force in my life. She encouraged me to continue college while I was in active duty. Nancy and I had known each other forever. We were childhood friends and had a permanent bond for the love we shared for our three children. Shortly after our divorce, we had a deep discussion walking on the beach about our relationship, our children and our extended family in Atlanta. We were determined to maintain a positive parental relationship and we were honestly able to do this. I am the father of three children with Nancy: Frazier Jr., Sandra, and Angela.

Frazier Ben Todd, Jr

My son Frazier Jr. was born at Fort McClellan, Alabama. He is a junior and also looks a lot like me. I have always been proud of his intellectual ability and his generous nature. His first wife's name is Dorothea, and his second wife's name is Loretta. His children are Denaya, Levonne, Cynthia, Frazier Ben Todd III and Tamia.

Sandra Todd Martin

Sandra is my first-born daughter. She was born while I was stationed at Fort McClellan in Alabama. Sandra is an outstanding woman. She is industrious, considerate and spends money wisely. Her passion is her full-time ministry as a pioneer in Jehovah's service. She is married to Robert Martin. She has one daughter, Jennifer and two grandchildren Genesis and Jordan Josiah.

Angela Todd Bohannon

The youngest of these three children from my first marriage, Angela, was born at Brook Army Medical Center in Texas, while I was doing battlefield maneuvers at Fort Sam Houston, in San Antonio, Texas. I received a message that said, "You are the father of a new baby girl." When I was able to return home, my wife and my new bundle of joy greeted me. Angela is kind and generous. She is the one that everyone approaches to converse. She retired from a big company in California. She too is now a full-time pioneer as a Jehovah's Witness. Angela is married to Noah Bohannon. Angela's children are Niah, Brigitte and Ronald. Her grandchildren are Isiah and Jordan Phillip.

I believe it is important to remember the pain of the other person when there is a divorce in the family; I experienced hurt and I believe my spouse Nancy did also. My children were very deeply affected. I learned that in a divorce, you lose some of the bonds with them because you are not there on a daily basis. I lost precious time with them; I worried about their health and everything. I remember during my pain I could hear my mother telling me that all will be well when I turn to God for comfort.

Thankfully, Nancy and I were able to retain our friendship after the divorce. She faithfully came to see my mother in Atlanta, whenever she (Nancy) would visit from San Francisco. I kept in contact with her (Nancy's) mother and sisters. I presented part of the eulogy at her father's funeral and her sister's funeral. We are still a part of the same family.

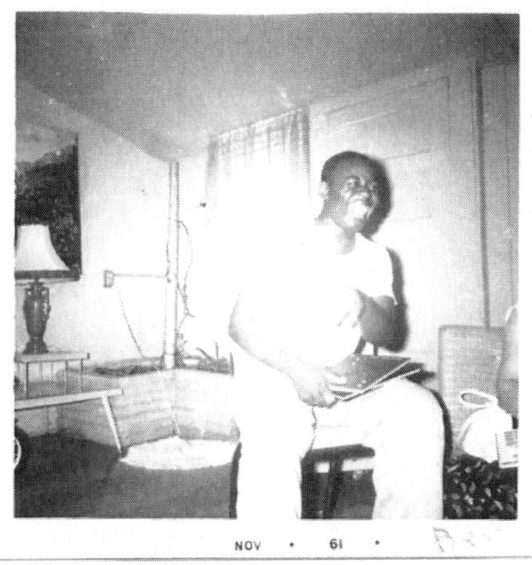

Frazier Sr., in San Antonio, TX, November 1961

Frazier Sr., second car-1957 Chevy.

Frazier Sr., first wife Nancy and children Sandra, Frazier Jr., 1960

Frazier Sr., first wife Nancy with children, Frazier Jr., Angela and Sandra 1962, Texas

Frazier Sr., with family, Nancy (children) Sandra, Angela, and Frazier Jr., in Japan 1964.

Frazier Sr., daughter-in-law, Dorothea (married Frazier Jr.) with grandchildren Jennifer, and Frazier III (BJ) Atlanta, 1987

The three Fraziers': Frazier Sr., Frazier Jr., and Frazier III (BJ), Atlanta, GA

Frazier Sr., with grandchildren Ronnie, Niah and Brigitte

Frazier Sr., with great grandchildren Genesis, Jordan Josiah (baby) and granddaughter, Jennifer (2018).

Frazier Sr., with granddaughter Niah at 2016 Todd-Smith family reunion.

Left to right: Frazier B. Todd Sr., with great grandchildren; Dylan, Dayana and Jaylan (front right). Grandchildren (Kobi and Tamia).

Frazier Sr., and great grandson Isaiah, Atlanta, GA 2013.

Frazier Sr., and granddaughter Bridgette, California.

Frazier Sr. and grandchildren. Left to right: granddaughter Cynthia, Levonne, grandson BJ, daughter Angela, son Emmanuel and granddaughter Niah. Atlanta, GA.

Frazier Sr.'s son, Frazier Jr., and granddaughters (left to right) Denaya, Cynthia and Levonne.

Frazier Sr.'s grandson Ronnie with family. Left to right: wife Miranda, Jordan Phillip and Isaiah (2017)

Frazier Sr., with youngest daughter, Angela (2018)

Frazier Sr., and daughter Sandra and granddaughter Jennifer, Atlanta, GA 2016.

Frazier Sr., with family. Left to right: sons-in-law: Robert, Noah, grandson in law Jerrard and Frazier Sr. Savannah, GA 2016

Frazier Sr., with daughters Angela and Sandra, California

Frazier Sr., First wife, Nancy Martin Todd Wood, California, 2018

CHAPTER 13
ACTIVE MILITARY DUTY

(1958-1967)

We did not have Reserved Officer Training Corps (ROTC) when I was in high school. I joined the U. S. Navy Reserve because I realized the military would help me further my education after high school. I attended high school at the same time I was in the Navy Reserve.

In the South, we were eager to join the military. I was in the Navy Reserve for two years (1956–1958). The Army Reserve and the Air Force would not allow African-American students in high school to join because there were no training camps in Georgia that accepted black students. Only the Navy Reserve accepted black high school students.

When I was in the Navy Reserve, other recruits and I would go to the Naval air stations in Norcross, Georgia, for their reserve duty and flying time training. On the weekends, white pilots would come in and fly us around. I loved to fly with them. That was the first time I rode in a big airplane. One of my duties in the Navy Reserve was to be a tail gunner. My job was to protect the rear of the Naval aircraft and shoot down any enemy that came to the rear of the plane.

Navy Reserve to Army

Early in 1958, (before I was married to Nancy), while I was at Morehouse College, an historical black college and university in Atlanta (HBCU), I had a conflict of scheduling. My chemistry lab class and Navy Reserve basic training were both scheduled on Saturday morning. I chose to go to my chemistry lab class. Therefore, I missed several Navy Reserve training dates. Then the Navy ordered me to report for active duty. I had a difficult decision to make. I wanted to stay in college, but the Navy had called me. That was the first time I ever violated a military principle. I went absent without leave, AWOL.

I came home from school one day and Mom said, "Son, the military police [MP] came to pick up your clothes from the Navy because you didn't report to active duty and they're looking for you." I knew I had to resolve this situation quickly.

I went down to see the Army recruiter on Ponce de Leon Avenue (Atlanta). I met with him and requested to join the Army. He looked at me and said, "Okay, but you have to take this test." I went in and took the test. He was shocked that I passed the test so easily. I told him I wanted to go to Chemical Warfare School after he explained I could continue my education in chemistry. At Chemical Warfare School, I was trained to protect the forces in the field and destroy the enemy with hazardous agents and substances, such as mustard gas and nerve gas. I did not tell him why I needed to be sworn in immediately. He told me that he could place me into a class. "Get me in today," I said urgently. He called his officer and I was sworn in that day.

Joining the Army helped me to resolve my problem with the Navy. My problem was that I had missed five weekends of training in my Reserve duties because I was attending my chemistry classes at Morehouse College on Saturday mornings. By joining the Army, I avoided the maximum punishment of dishonorable discharge, reduction of pay and confinement of five years. After I was sworn into the Army, I showed him the letter from the Navy. He said, "I knew it was too good to be true. A boy walks in off the street, aces my test, and gets into the Army. That just doesn't happen."

The Army recruiter called the Navy and told them that I was in the Army now and had already been sworn in. I had to be sworn in to have been accepted into the Army school system. I had to report that same day. He took me home to get my little suitcase, and then directly to the recruiting station on Ponce de Leon. I spent the night so the Navy would not come to my home and lock me up.

Basic Training - Words of Wisdom from Mom

My mom gave me the best piece of advice when I enlisted into the Army. She said, "Son, I'm going to tell you something now; it doesn't rain in the Army."

I laughed and said, "Mom, it rains everywhere."

She said, "Son, it doesn't rain in the Army; it rains on the Army."

That was the best advice I received because we did not cancel anything because of rain, sleet, snow, thunderstorm, or anything else. We lived in the field after the first two weeks of basic training in a tent. I completed my eight to ten weeks of basic training at Fort Chaffee, Arkansas.

Fort Chaffee, Arkansas

At nineteen years old, I was sent from my basic training base of Fort Chaffee, Arkansas, to Fort McClellan in Alabama. My basic training unit at Fort Chaffee was the C Battery Third Battalion Artillery Training Command. Fort McClellan was the Army Chemical Corps Headquarters. I was training in the chemical field. At my sign-up, I was to be a chemical laboratory technologist, but I was caught up in what they called "chemical warfare technology." I learned all the secrets of nerve gas and mustard gas, and how these chemicals could destroy the enemy and protect our troops.

Basic training was probably one of the most challenging things I have ever been involved in. I learned how to use a weapon, self-defense, how to kill the enemy, and defend the country. I felt that my skills were without boundaries. After going through rigorous training, the reward was twofold: I was a strong unstoppable defender.

Jammed Weapon

However, it was not all fine and dandy. Let us be clear: basic training is hard, tough work, and there is no rest for the weary. I had some narrow escapes in training in Fort Chaffee in 1958. Once, I was caught in a military barrage of artillery. I suffered with the permanent loss of some hearing in my left ear, and I almost accidently fired upon a friendly troop. That is called "friendly fire." I was caught behind with a jammed weapon as the "enemy" was approaching and firing.

In basic training each Army unit had mock battles of reality. This would include the artillery and infantry (foot soldier) training together. It may be ten people on your line and you had to advance together. Every three hundred to five hundred yards there were dummy soldiers that would pop up and we had to fire upon them and the artillery would shoot live ammunition over our heads. That is when my weapon jammed. They called a cease-fire so I would not hurt anyone in front of me—that is how soldiers are accidently killed all the time. That was a close call for me.

I remember the sergeant chewing me out for allowing my weapon to jam. I was just learning how to use it. Learning how to clear a weapon and how to un-jam it was an experience. We were taught how to open our weapons, dismantle them, and put them back together, and we could strip it while wearing blindfolds. We would open the rifle, take it off, clean it out, and put it back together in the dark because you could not use light in a combat situation. It was essential that we learn how to handle our weapons in darkness.

There were many more challenges in my military life. For instance, learning how to trust God for protection while sleeping in a field tent in the desert with poisonous rattlesnakes, scorpions, and other dangerous crawlers that could possibly slip into your bed tent. When the artillery was engaged at night, firing with the tracers round (visible bullets the Army used to name targets that were hit) flying over your head from the field artillery units, it was the grace of God that sustained me in all these areas.

Carrying Supplies

In the Army we had a roll-pack tent. It took two people to put the tent together. The poncho was used as a raincoat.

There was a special shovel that we used to dig foxholes (which is a hole in the ground used by the military as a shelter against enemy fire). We carried everything, such as a change of clothes and cooking utensils, in our pack, which weighed between sixty and seventy-five pounds. They trained us how to be soldiers night and day, 24/7, no matter the occasion.

Buddy Soldiers

Soldiers are well-informed and learn how to take care of themselves and their buddy in the field. If your buddy was wounded, you knew how to render first aid and bring your buddy out. If you were wounded, he would bring you out. That was the Army, and it was exciting. I was excited to learn these tasks, as well as experience the comradeship created with those men. Now, there are brave men and women who serve in the Army, but in the late fifties, around 1958 to 1959, it was only men who served in the combat unit.

Chemical Warfare Training

During the 1958 Lebanon crisis, we were put on high alert in case the enemy in that area used chemical warfare, including gas. The Lebanon crisis was a Lebanese uprising caused by religious and political disturbance in that country. One of the major concerns for the United States Department of Defense was protecting our military forces in the event of a chemical warfare attack.

I was reassigned to the United States Army 100th Chemical Group (COMMZ) as a Chemical Biological Radiological (CBR) Specialist for advance training to the chemical corps school in Anniston, Alabama (Fort McClellan) in 1958. After my extensive training in the chemical warfare department, I was assigned to the chemical battalion headquarters detachment as a CBR Specialist. My duty was to protect and save the lives of those harmed from chemical agents. This was a dangerous mission because the Army had to prepare to destroy the enemy in the event the enemy used dangerous gas to kill United States soldiers. At the same time, the Army had to protect the United States soldiers. Every soldier was issued a protective mask, a poncho that completely covered the body, and the syringe antidote atropine for nerve gas.

I went into chemical warfare school with the Army and learned how to be an effective chemical, biological, and radiological warfare specialist. I was an expert in generating smoke, mixing chemicals, and I was an expert with mustard gas and other agents. We never really needed that in the war, but nonetheless, the Army needed an expert, and I was one of them.

Chemical Practice

While it was important to know what the side effects were of certain chemicals produced, it was equally important to know exactly what to expect. Thus, as soldiers we practiced giving each other atropine injections. The atropine was designed to counter the effects of one possible nerve gas. One of the most frightening things I had to do was sit in a chair while I stuck the practice antidote in my thigh through my clothing. The training syringe had dextrose (sugar) in it. We had to leave it there until the instructors came and inspected.

At other times, during training we had to go into the gas chamber. It was very surreal. We wore an M9A1 gas mask. The mask would protect us against all known gases and chemicals at the time, except for nerve gas. Nerve gas could paralyze you and kill you unless you had the antidote. I was trained to administer the antidote for nerve gas.

When we entered the gas chamber, I felt nervous, my heart pounding, and I was anxious. The gas mask felt tight and claustrophobic. Once everyone was in the chamber and the door was sealed, the instructor ordered us to remove our masks. There would be five of us in there at a time. I ripped my mask off quickly, and once everyone had his mask off, we would have to stay in there for three minutes. It was the longest three minutes of my life! I felt like I was going to die! I felt like someone was strangling me. I was choking, I threw up, and the instructors just stood there watching us.

Then the instructors opened the door and let us come out. I was throwing up, the guys were sick and laying on the ground, and the instructors just carefully watched us. Then they said, "You see how the mask protects you from what you just went through?" That was a teaching moment! I always kept my M9A1 gas mask with me in top shape, always clean and ready. That experience with the real deal made a lasting impression.

Generate Smoke

The other thing I learned was how to generate smoke. There was a smoke machine that we could use for camouflage. It was used for cover so we could hide friendly troops from the enemy. Another aspect of my training was learning how to kill the enemy with a flamethrower (this weapon would literally project fire). I could carry this big flamethrower on my back and take it up to a cave, point it in there for forty-five to sixty seconds, and burn the enemy if they were hidden in a cave. That was a part of our job—protect our own soldiers from nerve gas, protect our own troops against gases, and be able to disperse and kill the enemy in case they used gas.

My first two years in the military were in the Chemical Corps. I specialized in top-secret and sensitive assignments. Therefore, I am not at liberty to discuss any other experiences. Let us just say that it was a riveting and educational experience.

Army Musician

In 1960, I decided that I did not want to be a support troop in the chemical biological radiological warfare area. Although I had fallen in love with the military, I wanted to save lives rather than destroy them. The Army allowed me to be reassigned to the US Army 296th Army Band located at Fort McClellan because they were in need of more trumpet musicians. I auditioned for the band and became an Army musician for a short period (about six months). I was accepted and it was there that I decided to make a military career. I transferred out and became an Army musician until my enlistment was completed.

In 1960, I was sent to Ft. Jackson, South Carolina for a three-month course in music school. Later I was assigned to the 440 Army Band in Fort Bragg, North Carolina.

In 1961, I was leaning toward getting a PhD or becoming a teacher or even a professor, but I applied to become a medical technologist. I passed all the tests, even the colorblind test. I do not know how I got through that test because I am colorblind. I had to serve in the military a period of three years for that training.

The Medical Field Service Schools, which helped doctors make diagnosis, had openings all over and were short on medical technologists. I was not sure what a medical technologist was, but when I went to the hospital and saw how involved, they were and that they helped the doctors make diagnosis, I knew in my heart that I had to be in the medical field.

San Antonio

I went to Texas in 1961 for a course called Medical Basic Technology. I really enjoyed that class. One of the subjects in medical technology is basic algebra. Some of the students were weak in math. In the medical field, I was well versed in math because I was an honor student with math in high school.

The math classes were easier for me in military school. Math was my strongest subject and I was happy to help other students who asked for help. "In basic training I had learned we are one. We help each other because we are united together to do this." If a student was weak in math, I would sit down and go over the basic algebra principle with him or her, or another subject in chemistry or in serology. If I was weak in a subject, someone would tutor me. It was important to me to support my classmates

All my classmates in the Army tech class passed because we were there for each other. I passed all my classes, such as chemistry, biology, parasitology, hematology, microbiology, and serology. No one in our group failed. In those four months, I became a medical technologist. My first assignment was at Fort Sam Houston, Texas, at the Medical Field Service School to the 67th medical group.

Medical Group

The 67th was a combat-ready crew that had to go to the field and set up a hospital of 250 beds and be ready to receive patients within two to four hours wherever the mission was, anywhere in the world. That is what we were set up to do, and we were trained for that continuously. However, those of us who had special skills would go over to the hospital. I worked there on a regular basis to keep my skill levels up and to care for patients. The doctors, of course, were not assigned to the field; they stayed in the hospital. As a medical tech, I was a soldier first, then a specialist.

My First Job in Korea.

My first job in Korea was as an non-commissioned officer in charge (NCOIC) of a medical lab, a general dispensary, which was right next to the hospital (U.S. Army Hospital in Ascom City, Korea). The Army had a huge laboratory. The hospital took care of all the sexually transmitted diseases (STD). I was given the nickname by locals as the "pussy doctor."

All of the women who came in that were infected were treated and given a card stating that they were free of any STD. In this way, the Army was taking care of the soldiers (GIs).

My military heroes were generals in the military, such as General Dwight D. Eisenhower and General MacArthur. General Eisenhower was the thirty-fourth president of the United States (1953–1961). He was also a five-star general in the United States Army during World War II and served as Supreme Commander of the Allied forces in Europe. General Douglas MacArthur was also a five-star general. He was Chief of Staff in the US Army in the 1930s. He oversaw issues in the Pacific theater during WWII. They were men of courage leading us to victory during WWII.

I always knew there might be a chance that I would be deployed in real combat, and this happened in 1965. I looked to my military heroes, as well as called upon God to watch over me and my buddies. Too many of my comrades and buddies did not return from the war zone. I remember them even as I served in various departments during my time in the Vietnam theater of operations.

Vietnam Theater of Operations

My first job in the Vietnam theater of operations was in 1965, at the 406 Medical Lab in Tokyo, Japan, as the NCOIC of the Veterinary Medical Department. It was there that I had a chance to travel to conduct the military's missions and tasks.

I was a medical technologist (specialist who helps doctors make diagnosis) and non-commissioned officer in charge (NCOIC) of the Hematology Department 106 General Hospital. My service in the medical department as a medical technologist of the US Army in the Vietnam theater of operations was quite taxing, and tears come to my eyes sometimes when I talk about it.

My job was to keep our comrades repaired, keep soldiers fighting, and keep all who served alive. When I saw wounded soldiers, I made sure they were comfortable by prescribing medication, and before they returned to their families, I supplied services for their emotional state and documentation of disease-free health.

One of my responsibilities in the Vietnam theater of operations was to verify that the food and water supply was safe for the military to consume. I am unable to give those details, I would leave our home base in the Vietnam theater of operations on a Monday, fly out with the Air Force, who would take our unit where we needed to go, and they would bring us back on a Thursday. We did that for a little over a year. I was following the orders given by the president of the United States, Lyndon B. Johnson. I focused on keeping my fellow brothers and myself safe from harm and protecting our liberties.

Around 1966, I was at the 106 General Hospital in Yokohama, Japan, which was my last job on active duty in the Vietnam theater of operations. As the chief medical laboratory specialist, I examined laboratory specimen such as blood, stool, sputum, urine, and other body fluids to authenticate that the soldiers were disease-free and could leave the Vietnam theater of operation.

One of my jobs was to make sure the soldiers did not return to the States with malaria or any other disease that could be contagious, including sexually transmitted diseases (STD) or other tropical disorders.

I served as the NCOIC of the hematology department, which was responsible for the safety of all military personnel in the Vietnam theater of operations, ensuring they received a malaria screen before returning to America. This too was an awesome responsibility. The United States did not need a malaria epidemic back on the mainland. After I was in this unit one month, I received my much-deserved promotion to E-6.

Implicit Racial Bias in the Military

President Truman issued an executive order that integrated the Armed forces in 1948. This was after World War II and just before the Korean War.

As a young black man growing up in the South, I had a clear understanding of the Jim Crow laws of segregation during this period. Upon arriving at Fort Chaffee, Arkansas, I was amazed to see how integrated my basic training unit was. I was also surprised how the activities on all the Southern military bases showed signs of integration until I left that installation and entered another world off the military base. There is one implicit racial bias experience I will never forget in the military.

The commissioned officer, a veterinarian, had not arrived within the command and would not be available for one year. The department managed monitoring the quality of all foods, milk products, water supplies, research, and responding to all the known and unknown tropical diseases that might affect our troops directly or indirectly. This was an impressive task. There were more than one hundred professionals assigned to this department at this large research and support laboratory. This was one of the largest Research and Development Laboratory for the Department of Defense outside of the continental United States.

The incidence that I recall of implicit racial bias occurred after I received the rank of E-5, a mid-level rank of authority within the Armed forces. I was a leader equivalent to a mid-level manager in the civilian world. This rank shows that I was qualified to perform my work with skill and ability, and lead and direct others. Currently, I was at the 67th of the Medical Group Field Hospital at Fort Sam Houston, Texas, in 1962. It was an exceedingly difficult time for me. While in an overseas command in Vietnam, I was a soldier, in the pay grade of E-5, promotable to the next pay grade, E-6. A white captain expressed his bias and held that prejudiced opinion until I was transferred out of the lab. I had a prior unpleasant encounter with this captain at a company social event. The captain appeared inebriated and was using profanity in front of my wife Nancy. I stood and respected his rank and told him to respect my wife. The captain got very red and continued to use derogatory words. My wife and I left the event. He later made the statement to me "You will never get promoted in this unit". I felt this was racially motivated as I ran the department in a pay grade slot of E-5 for one year with marked efficiency.

One day, an executive officer called me into his office and said to me, "Specialist Todd, we have a new man coming into the unit to assist you. Teach him everything you know about your job, and then you both will compete for the promotion." I saluted and left his office. I knew that I would not be promoted in this unit, even though I had many commendations for my job performance.

I remember when I received a written letter of commendation for personally organizing and delivering to the Air Force plane an emergency request for thousands of units of blood for our soldiers. In addition, around 1961-1962 while serving in the 24TH Evacuation Hospital, San Antonio, TX I received a letter of commendation for outstanding service to my unit. My original military training was with the U.S. Army Chemical Corp. as mentioned earlier. I was a well-trained military chemical specialist before I went to the U.S. Army Medical Corps. The unit did not have a CBR Commissioned Officer, I had to serve as the NCOIC in addition to my regular medical service for the unit. While my unit was engaged in a regular 72-hour

ATT, Army training test which included having judges-empires-officers from headquarters grading our unit performance during the test of endurance. I along with my unit engaged in 72-hours without sleep-rest and in full operation under assimilated combat conditions was quite enduring and challenging. A simulated atomic bomb was exploded in the combat zone. In this scenario our hospital unit was in the fall-out zone. I was called to the unit headquarters for a briefing and advice about our position and possible effect of the downwind atomic fall-out with contamination to our unit, personnel and equipment. I was able with confidence to calculate on the big battle field map and predict with accuracy the amount of time our unit would have before we had to break down the 250 bed hospital, pack up, load up, and relocate to a safe zone and still provide medical services to the combat units in the battle zone. Because of my training, I was able to perform my job as needed with confidence. Soon after, I was promoted to my then current position of grade of Specialist E-5 for my over-all job performance as CBR trainer and Medical Laboratory Specialist. The Army paid a Specialist an extra $60.00 a month to remain enlisted in the service. For these reasons I felt that I was the best qualified because of my education and experience.

The new soldier was a white man, a particularly good man. After he realized the enormous responsibilities, he said to me, "You are the one that deserves any promotion in this department." He then voluntarily went to another unit. His request was granted.

It was not until I was transferred to my new unit, the new hospital commander advanced me ahead of the line and I was promoted to the pay grade of E-6 within sixty days. This was at 106 General Hospital in Yokohama, Japan.

The Vietnam theater of operations included Southeast Asia. I had worked extremely hard in support of our forces in the battle zone. The promotion gave me a new insight into the life of many of my comrades in arms and what some of them had to endure to have a successful military career. I was thankful I was able to overcome the many forms of racism that I personally experienced.

Operation Desert Storm

It was a privilege to serve my country in the Army Reserves during Operation Desert Storm around 1990–1991. I was deployed from Atlanta to Fort Steward, Georgia. I performed procedures on the soldiers returning with lower extremity injuries. I would gladly take the call again today. I love my country. I am honored to have served in the U.S. military for twenty-six years.

Every experience in my life has been a stepping-stone—not an obstacle—to another level of wisdom, knowledge, and understanding. Every step I took in my military career was a stepping-stone to my civilian career. Every step in my civilian career was a stepping-stone to my military career.

For example, I was able to stay in touch with some of my military buddies. One of the pilots, John, who flew our team to different places, worked for the Central Intelligence Agency (CIA). He became my neighbor when I lived in East Point, Georgia. Jack, a Christian man and a great friend, encouraged me through some of the difficult times in my life. It was in military where I began to understand the value of lifelong friendship.

I learned many life lessons from the military. The military taught me structure and order. That order is headship, leadership, character building, and building blocks. I depended on my buddies as they depended on me, particularly in the fox hole. The military is designed as a fighting machine to protect our country.

The Medical Corps Department keeps the fighting men fighting and physically and emotionally stable to protect their families.

Frazier Sr., U. S. Army Basic Training 1958, Ft Chappee, Arkansas

Frazier B. Todd Sr., Left second row standing. Twelfth Chemical (Entry) Class June 9th-August 9th 1958.

Frazier Sr., receiving Army military promotion.

Frazier B. Todd, Sr., posing in his U. S. Army uniform, Operation Desert Storm,

Major Frazier B. Todd, Sr., at home- dress for a picture in his U. S. Army uniform post Operation Desert Storm, Atlanta, GA 1991.

CHAPTER 14
MEDICAL SCHOOL

After Military Career

This chapter will discuss why I chose the medical field and highlight my challenges in medical school. As I have come to understand my destiny, I now realize that God placed me in different areas in preparation for where I am today.

When I was younger, I always loved math—especially in high school and in college. In high school, I had taken algebra 1, 2, 3 and advanced algebra. After that, I took geometry. I loved trigonometry. I had great schooling in all areas of math.

After basic training, I attended the Chemical Corps School in Alabama, where I obtained knowledge about military combat use of chemical warfare. Upon completion, I was able to attend the Medical Field Service School. This period was an intensive sixteen weeks of college course medical training to equip me to be a qualified medical technologist (a medical technologist runs blood test, urine analysis and the drawing of blood after many tests). Active duty in the Army allowed me to complete my education, travel, and see the world. That was the beginning of my career path, and while I did not fully know it at the time, I would embark on my journey in the medical field.

Around 1961–1962, I attended San Antonio University while stationed at the U.S. Army Science Academy in Texas. At each of my military assigned stations, I was able to continue my college education. I was determined to earn my college degree.

From 1967 through 1972, I worked in the lab at the Presbyterian Medical Center (the name was later changed to Pacific Medical Center), which was a part of the Stanford University Hospital residency program. I worked at night as a medical technologist and attended school full-time during the day. A medical technologist is a specialist who helps doctors make diagnosis. A medical technologist's responsibility is keeping a high caliber of accuracy for blood tests and lab results so that doctors can make the right diagnosis. Each medical center, including the military, had teaching centers. At the medical centers, young doctor residents became seasoned physicians.

At that point, in my career, I realized that I could be a doctor because I had the potential knowledge. I decided to pursue medical school. At the time, I was the medical laboratory supervisor of the evening shift from 3:00 p.m. to 11:00 p.m. I was accepted into the California College of Podiatric Medicine in San Francisco, California, with a full tuition scholarship (GI Bill). I completed my degree in four years. It was one of the most difficult things I have ever done. My father lost his leg from diabetes; this inspired me to specialize in podiatric medicine.

Starting in 1963, while stationed in San Francisco, I attended the Advanced Medical Technology Military Medical School course at Lettermen General Hospital. This advanced, fifty-week course was the equivalent of a master's degree in basic science. I earned my first Bachelor of Science degree upon successfully completing my first year of medical school. My early Army training in medical technology afforded me the opportunity to have a career in medicine.

In 1968, my first week of medical school was particularly challenging. I will never forget my professor of anatomy, Dr. George Reise. He taught with both facial expressions and his hands.

During the first day's lecture, he blew me away with his knowledge. I thought I knew anatomy, but I realized I had a lot to learn. The next day, Dr. Reise gave the class a pop quiz. He gave a quiz every day, which meant I had to study every night for that one class.

I had seven classes every day. I took anatomy and physiology, which were difficult classes. The other courses were general and basic orthopedics, physical diagnosis, and general medicine. All the courses were challenging.

I had exams or quizzes in every class every day. I had to stay up and study at night. I was determined to make it through my first semester, so I would study four hours every day. I was the second-oldest person in the class. The younger students who had just gotten out of college went straight into medical school. I had been out of high school ten years before I decided to attend medical school in 1968. At the time, I had three children with my first wife Nancy.

My goal in going into the medical field was to provide pain and relief from a spiritual and physical point of view.

The first semester of medical school was brutal. I remember trying to work nights at the hospital lab prior to going to medical school. I went to work after the first week and told the pathologist I worked for, Dr. Burns, "I can't do this and go to medical school." It was extremely hard to work nights and go to medical school during the day.

He said, "We knew it, we've already set aside a day job for you."

Dr. Burns made me the weekend supervisor, which meant I worked from Saturday morning at 7:00 a.m. until 3:00 p.m. Sunday evenings at the Pacific Medical Center in California. My pay was a full salary for working those hours, and it is something I will always be thankful for. I had that job for four years. I was fortunate to earn a full salary while attending school. Over the course of four years, I dealt with long hours in the classroom, the labs, student rotations in the clinical areas of the different medical specialists, and hours upon hours of study and preparation with little rest or sleep.

Frazier Sr., San Francisco California College of Podiatric Medicine yearbook 1970.

Frazier Sr., (1st row – 4th from the left) 1969 Medical School, San Francisco, CA.

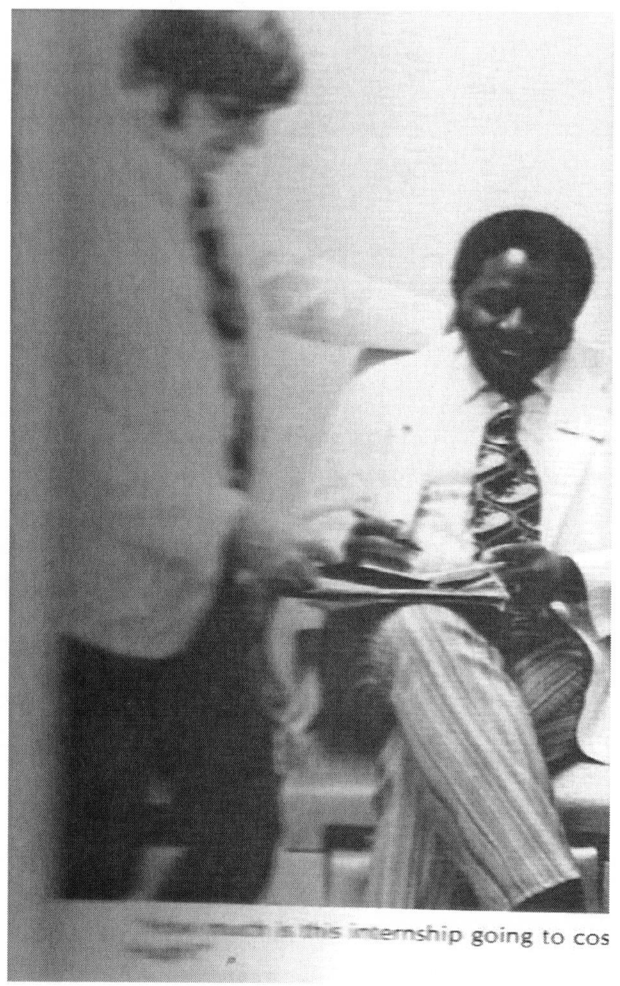

Frazier Sr., candid picture from the last year in medical school, California

FRAZIER BEN TODD, B.S, D.P.M.
Atlanta, Georgia
Morehouse College
University of San Francisco
C.C.P.M., B.S.
American Society of Medical Technologists
A.P.S.A.
Community Medicine
U.C. and C.C.P.M. Home Care 4
Chairman Minority Student Recruitment Committee
A.G.K. Fraternity 1, 2, 3, 4
A.G.K. Fraternity Vice-President 3
Class Treasurer 2

Hey Ben - you look just like you did in 1972 - keep up the good work -
Ron Uhlman
7/24/87

Frazier, Sr., 1972 Medical School graduation picture, California

CHAPTER 15
MY SECOND LOVE, TERUMI

In 1966, I was a non-commissioned officer in charge of the Department of Veterinarian Medicine at 406 Medical Lab (at that time it was the largest research laboratory outside the United States.) The lab had everything within that department, including many different chemicals, so I had to be incredibly careful. I had 150 in-house personnel reporting to me from the Veterinarian Medicine Department and in Research and Development. We were the Research and Development Lab, where we had civilian veterinarians and civilian technicians from different countries working for the United States government and helping us find answers and solutions to the different parasites, hematoma, fevers, and so forth, for Southeast Asia.

One day, this four foot-eight-inch-tall young Japanese women, Terumi (who worked at the medical laboratory) came into the office. She held out her hand and blood dripped from her finger. A rat had bitten her finger, or she had stuck a needle in her finger; I do not recall the exact details. She did not speak much English, but my Japanese was good so we could communicate. I brought her up to my office, filled out an incident report, which were reported stateside, and she was treated medically. I told her that I needed to see her in a week to see how the wound was healing. That was our first meeting. We later became colleagues and developed a working friendship at the laboratory.

Around 1967, I was 28 years old and had returned to the United States. In 1968, Terumi graduated from Kitasato University in Tokyo, Japan, and received a Bachelor of Science degree in Medical Technology. After Terumi finished college, she often wrote me. She let me know she had been accepted at a graduate university in San Francisco, California. She was excited to come to America to work on her master's degree. I was living in San Francisco, and Terumi wrote me to let me know she was coming to America.

Upon her arrival to America, she contacted me. I picked her up from the airport and took her over to the university. I was the only person she knew in the States in that department. Our friendship grew and we became romantically involved. After dating for about three months-I became more attracted to her. I loved her accent. She was an exquisite classical guitarist and an auto harp specialist too. She had a beautiful singing voice. We really hit it off. Terumi had a career that matched mine; she was a medical technologist. She was committed to helping me complete medical school. My children from my first marriage (Nancy) spent time with her. I decided to settle down with her. I picked her up one day and said, "Let's get married." She said ok, and that was our beginning. Terumi and I were married in 1968 at the San Francisco courthouse. We spent our honeymoon on Broadway in San Francisco, California. I was happy to know that Terumi wanted to have children with me.

Ado Terushi Todd

My first son with Terumi is Ado Terushi Todd. His middle name, Terushi, he shares with his grandfather, Terushi Kuroshima. Ado was born in 1971 in San Francisco, at the University of California Medical Center. At that time, I was in medical school training. The medical school doctors and students made a bet with me to predict the exact time Ado would be born. Happily, I won the bet.

Ado is highly intelligent, always at the top of his class on the honor roll. School was just easy for him. He attended college, and is now the owner of his own pool company. Ado married Adrienne. His children are Kia, Akio, and Ory.

Dr. Tobi Todd

My son Tobi was born in 1973 at South Fulton Medical Center (now called Atlanta Medical Center South / WellStar South). He followed my example and graduated from the same medical school as I did.

In 2003, Tobi took over my medical practice when I retired. I had the opportunity to work with Tobi in complex surgical procedures. Tobi is a very caring man with his family and patients. Tobi's middle name Floyd comes from my father. He is married to Angelyca, and their daughter's name is Kobi.

Emmanuel Gabriel Todd

Terumi and I were living in Atlanta when our youngest son, Emmanuel Gabriel, was born in 1980. He was born nine months after a romantic trip to Europe that included Paris and

London. I named him Emmanuel, which means "messenger of God," because of his difficult birth. We almost lost Emmanuel, as well as Terumi, at his birth.

On the day Terumi went into labor with Emmanuel, I had just finished doing multiple corrective lower extremities surgical procedures at another Atlanta Hospital Medical Center. I returned to the hospital where Terumi was in labor, and her OB-GYN physician was a particularly good friend of mine. His office was across the street from where I practiced on Stone Hogan Road in Atlanta in the same medical complex. The physician told me later that it seemed her delivery would be difficult and dangerous. We talked about the options and he thought a C-section would be okay, but he would rather wait until later.

At the last minute, he told me it was too late for a C-section. The baby was too large for her area because she was a small woman, about four-eight and weighed about 120 pounds. Terumi had gained forty pounds when pregnant with Emmanuel. I was there for the delivery.

Emmanuel Gabriel weighed ten pounds and was the largest baby that we had had. He was born cyanotic (bluish in color due to lack of oxygen), and was rushed to the infant intensive care unit (ICU.) My family and the members of my church congregation (Davis Chapel AME) prayed for them. He was in intensive care (ICU) for two weeks before the doctors would allow Terumi to see him. I saw him every day. A week later, before they were both discharged to go home, I named Emmanuel at the hospital. "God is with you, Gabriel. You're an angel, and you have to have a special anointing on your life."

When Emmanuel was three weeks old, I prayed and baptized him by throwing him in the swimming pool at our home. Terumi was shocked and stunned, but that was his baptism into life. He started swimming on that very day. He's been swimming ever since. At the time of this writing, Emanuel has not married or had any children. He is a diligent worker. He graduated from Morehouse College in Atlanta and works with his brother Ado.

The Divorce

Terumi and I enjoyed a comfortable life and it was a delight raising our three boys together. After twenty-five years of marriage, I was blindsided when Terumi wanted a divorce. We had taken a trip to Hawaii and stopped in San Francisco to see Sandra, Angela, and Tobi (who was in medical school.) A month after our return, she said she wanted to pursue her music career and she felt I would not allow her to. She said that our boys were grown now. This was her time. She no longer wanted to be a doctor's wife. Thinking back, there were signs that I did not see. We went to counseling however; it did not help. She moved downstairs into the guest room, prepared my meals, and was my wife in every aspect but marital intimacy for two years.

Her parents had recently died I thought she was going through a depression because of the death of her parents. I had hoped that I would be able to fill the void. I spent many evenings talking on the phone with my daughters (Sandra and Angela) in California. They sent me Bible-based articles to read about marriage, in addition I was in spiritual conversations with my bishop at COHM. My daughters stressed the need to put Terumi first, before other family members. I felt that I always had. I think that was a big part of how she had felt over the years. She had a highly active role in our ministry as a praise and worship person at the Church of Hope Ministry (COHM). She would always sing a solo just before I delivered the message in our church for the television program in the Atlanta area, which was extremely popular. I felt she was happy expressing her art in the ministry. However, I failed because Terumi did not feel she came first.

Terumi was the one I was supposed to retire with and see the world. Twenty-five years is a lifetime. I was devastated emotionally. I had to live with the guilt that I had not been the husband she needed. I felt shame that we were not the perfect family I thought we were. After the divorce I was very lonely and secretly hoped we would get back together. I had not realized how much I had grown to love her. I shed many tears during this time.

Soon after the divorce, I went on a date with a significant other. I coincidently saw Terumi while out on the date. She got so angry with me. She said, "I thought you would wait for me." I realized that at this point our relationship was over. It took me years to move forward emotionally and to have peace. As with my first wife Nancy, Terumi and I have a family-based relationship that allows us to support each other.

In marriage, I feel each mate should always come first in the other person's life. I should have never assumed that she knew it. I should have worked harder so that in her heart she knew that she was first with me.

Mom (Mary Alice) visits California

While married to Terumi and living in California, I finished medical school (1972). Many of my family members came out to visit me, including my mother. That was one of the highlights of my life.

She came to California to be with us at the graduation, which was the farthest she had ever flown. Terumi and I drove her up the coastline on Highway 1 up into the mountains. She saw the Golden Gate Bridge and the Sequoia trees. We even took her to Mexico.

* * *

This is a little joke on the side. My brother Larry, the baby boy, was always jealous of Mom and any interest other men may have had in her. Larry did not want any man around Mom after my father's death. While she was in California visiting Terumi and me-I told Larry that I had set up a date for her (pretend) and boy did Larry get upset! He called me up and told me to make her come home.

* * *

Other times, Mom would be out with the girls and having a great time. A highlight for her was eating at a restaurant that looked over the ocean. She had never had that experience before—eating a meal while watching the ocean waves. Our home was in Pacifica, California, right off the seashore. You could sit and look out our window and watch the sunset every day. You could see the sunset as it was going down into the ocean. It was a beautiful view, and she would sit in the window when the sunset and just smile. It was one of the joys in my life to see Mom do that.

Mom saw all of this before she died in 1991. She was living in Atlanta when she passed. She reminisced about California and just smiled and said she wished my dad, Floyd Todd, could have been in California with her to see those sunsets. My mother, Mary Alice Smith Todd, was a wonderful, kind, and loving person until the end. She called all of us into her room at South Fulton Medical Center in East Point, which is now WellStar South, and said, "It's time for me to leave. Stop praying for me because I'm ready to go." Mary Alice transitioned on August 6, 1991. God bless Mary Alice.

Frazier Sr., mother, Mary Alice Smith Todd, in the 1970's, Atlanta, GA.

Frazier Sr. and second wife Terumi 1968

Frazier Sr., with second wife Terumi, 1993

Frazier Sr., with second wife Terumi and his mother-in-law, Hanako Kuroshima.

Frazier Sr., and family. Left to right: Ado, Emmanuel, Tobi and Terumi, Atlanta 1980

Frazier Sr., with children, Ado, Tobi and Emmanuel, 1983

Frazier Sr., wearing dashiki (colorful garment for women and men worn mostly in West Africa) hand sewn by second wife, Terumi.

Frazier Sr., grandsons Left to right: Akio, Ory and Kai. Far right son; Ado.

Frazier Sr., and grandson Kai.

Frazier Sr., with great granddaughter, Genesis and granddaughter Kobi 2013.

Frazier Sr.'s grandchildren (left to right) Kai, Ory and Akio.

Frazier Sr., second wife Terumi with grandchildren left to right: Kai, Ory and Akio.

Family members at the graduation of Tobi Todd from medical school, California

CHAPTER 16
MY LIFE AS A BACHELOR

San Francisco

In February 1967, I arrived from the Orient (Vietnam theater of operation) in preparation to go to San Francisco for my discharge from Army active duty. This was two years after Nancy, and I had divorced. I was discharged as a non-commissioned officer (NCO) with a grade of Specialist E-6.

Upon my first night of civilian life in San Francisco, I made a trip to Fillmore Street and found one of my favorite eating spots. I was starving for some good soul food, so I ordered a plate of pork ribs and a sweet potato pie. Wow! I will never forget that meal. I ate very slowly and breathed in the fresh air of life after my experiences in the Vietnam theater of operations—no restrictions of my movement, nor of my sleeping hours. I worked on getting used to it and at the same time I was looking forward to it.

I made a call to my ex-wife Nancy and paid a visit to her home. I was happy to see my children, Frazier, Sandra, and Angela. It had been two years since I had seen them. Later that night, I found a temporary hotel for me to rest in and adjust to the time zone change. The following Monday morning I made the pre-arranged appointment to the Pacific Medical Center to sign the contract for my old job in the clinical laboratory. It was a dream come true. The manager knew my aspirations, and again made me the night supervisor of the laboratory so I could attend college in the mornings, which I was able to do.

San Francisco in 1967 had been widely known as the summer of love or free love. Mostly young people fashioned the hippie lifestyle. As a young man in the workplace, I had a huge choice of women to date. The female nursing staff would come to the lab on a regular basis to have their special requests fulfilled by one of the three black men working in the lab on the night shift (myself and two other men.) One of the other men in the lab was also in preparation for medical school at Stanford University. He graduated a year after me from medical school. He would become a successful pathologist and worked for the Red Cross until his premature death. The last male has since retired; we still communicate via Facebook.

My life as an unmarried man in San Francisco was extremely exciting, yet stressful. It was a player's paradise. However, because of my background with the STDs overseas, I practiced safe sex.

The females outnumbered the men. My bachelor apartment was in Twin Peaks, a beautiful area of the city with an impressive view. One of my Army buddies, the late John Jackson, a black man who reached the highest rank Sergeant-Major E-9 in the Vietnam theater of operations, retired and shared this unit with me until he was married. He later served as the vice president of a leading bank in California. We all called him J.J., and he was a brilliant man with numbers and organizational structures.

1967 The Gun Clicked

One night, I stayed overnight at a nurse's home I knew from the hospital where I worked. I woke up with a gun to my head. She told me she had been divorced for several years, but her ex-husband had something else to say about it. That night, when her ex-husband held that gun to my forehead, I thought my life was over. I quickly said my prayers and explained to him that she had told me she was not married. He said, "I know." Then he lowered the weapon. I dressed so fast and left. I broke a world record on getting out of bed naked, putting on my underwear and socks, my pants, and then gathered my shirt and shoes and bolted out of the door toward my car, leaving behind the aroma of my shaving lotion.

When I arrived at my apartment, I prayed and made many promises to God—some I was able to keep, and some I later broke. Even though that was a scary situation, I was glad we were both safe.

Personal Escort

I had moved from San Francisco in the 1970s to Atlanta. I was an unmarried man again after Terumi, and I divorced in 1994 in Atlanta. The females in Atlanta were professional, with different aspirations, great jobs, and wealth.

One day, a woman came to my office. She was from New Jersey. My office manager came to my back office to tell me that I had a visitor who wanted to see me, but not as a patient. My manager had a big smile on her face.

Upon entering the front waiting room with patients looking on with excitement, the woman laid her credentials on the desk, her bank statement, and credit cards. She was the business owner of a nightclub. She smiled and simply said, "I understand that you are a bachelor. I travel to Atlanta often on business matters. I would like you to be my personal escort when I am in the city. I will take care of all the expenses. Are you interested?" This dumbfounded me. Wow, what an opportunity! I declined, however. At that time, my hands were already full trying to be a good Christian, family-oriented person, and a good example to my children and the world.

I recall another event that involved another patient (this occurred in 1995 or 1996). She was a post-surgical patient of several months, wearing shoes without any complaints. My office staff told her that my office was closing. She said in a loud voice to me when I entered the waiting room, "When are going to give me some?" I grunted in reply, embarrassed. She simply said, "You know what I want." I told her the office was closed and that she had to leave the building so my staff could go home. She left the office without incident.

However, I was not prepared for the episodes that followed that night. Unknowingly, she followed me to my home and waited a period of time. I was living alone in the home that Terumi and I shared before she moved out. The doorbell rang repeatedly. I checked the security system and recognized that she had followed me from the office to my residence. I called my lawyer for advice; she heard the banging on the door and the bell. My lawyer recommended that I should call the police, and I needed to have two witnesses of the experience. I then placed a call to my ex-wife Terumi and she, too, heard the commotion. She told me to call the police too. I placed the call to the local police department. When she saw the officers, she left.

My life as an unmarried man was exciting; however, it had its share of surprises.

CHAPTER 17
MY THIRD LOVE, ROBERTA

Roberta

Roberta is my third and very last wife. I knew her formally as a patient, and mostly when our children were young in school. They were former classmates in a local Atlanta private school. During, the 1970's and 1980's, I often saw her at the children's football games. Roberta and I were reacquainted in 1998. I realized that she was in my life for a good reason.

She came into my life through a friend of hers who suggested we make contact since we were both single at the time. She was divorced from a local Atlanta pastor. By the time we became reacquainted her two sons (who are pastors) and my six children were all adults.

I will never forget the first time I saw her. Her smile and her eyes sparkled. I was impressed when I first met Roberta. I admired her character and the way she dressed. Roberta always dressed upscale. One time I saw her elegantly styled beautiful grayish-colored hair in curls, and she wore a black, sexy dress that got my attention.

After we began dating and having regular Sunday dinner visits to her home with her family, her two sons asked me for a conference. Pastor Jasper Williams III and Dr. Joseph Williams directed me to an office in the home. I was aware of the impending interrogation of my plans for their mother, Roberta.

Pastor Jasper III affectionately asked me to sit down and began questioning me about my intentions for their mother. They asked, since their mother and I had been a couple for a few years, were we considering getting married. They reminded me of the Scriptures, and the biblical standard for an adult relationship between males and females.

I had considered this subject; however, I was not certain if either she or I were ready for until death do us part. At this point, I was moving forward after the divorce from Terumi, and I was afraid to make that commitment. After much deliberation with the two young men, I began to process the idea more and more in my spirit.

Later, Roberta called me and asked me to ride with her to the local 24-hour post office. She came by my home, picked me up and she asked me, "Where is our relationship going?"

We had been dating for a considerable time and it was time to make the final commitment to her. Her strength and calm manner were a balm to my soul. I am still not sure of what my reply was, however, I realized that God had placed a godly woman in my life for a reason. I began to seek his will, and he gave me his answer: *Roberta will make you a beautiful godly home and a wife until death do you part. She will be an asset in building the ministry.*" That was my answer. After much prayer and discussing the matter with my adult children and several of my adult granddaughters, I felt confident to ask Roberta for her hand in marriage. We went on a trip to San Francisco to meet my daughters, Sandra and Angela. I left Roberta with my daughters, who questioned her for what seemed to her three hours. When I came back, she was so glad to see me!

My daughters, like her sons, wanted a good person for their parent. This visit of approval by my girls was a defining moment for me. My girls often tell me how much they love Roberta. They are happy with Roberta because she has brought joy back into my life.

After our visit with my daughters, I wanted Roberta to see the hilly San Francisco area. As I was driving down the steep hill on a street named Fillmore, it seemed like I was going to drive into the ocean. Roberta would grab the car and hold on for dear life. She thought we were going to run into the ocean. It was exciting only because I knew there was really no danger, and secretly, she knew it too.

The Marriage Proposal

After our trip, I proposed to her in Douglasville, Georgia. We were looking for a house because Roberta's house was up for sale. After we saw a beautiful house that Roberta liked, I went and bought her a ring and proposed to her in that house. I took her hand, took the ring out, and asked her to marry me. She was ecstatic, and accepted my proposal. However, I did not buy the house. After we were married, we lived in an apartment called Village on the Green in Atlanta. Then I bought our home in Camp Creek Market Place, College Park, Georgia.

We were married in an outdoor setting in a gazebo at the Village on the Green found on Continental Colony Parkway. Her two pastor sons performed the intimate garden ceremony. Roberta's granddaughter was the flower girl. All our children were there except my daughters in California.

The Honeymoon

Jordan, Roberta's first granddaughter, age four, wanted to spend the night with us on our honeymoon. Her dad, Jasper Williams III, told her, not this night. Our honeymoon was in Europe and we were there for a week. First, we were in London, and then we went to Paris. It felt good to fall in love again. I was excited. On our honeymoon, it was an adventure because Roberta does not like to go underwater. I gave her a couple glasses of wine to prepare her for the trip under the English canal from England to Paris. She did much better on the return trip, just squeezing my hand. We had a lot of fun.

My Beautiful Supporter

I am an ordained minister. I have pastored COHM since 1985. Roberta supports me in the ministry.

Roberta had been married to a pastor before; she understood the stress that comes with a ministry. She had a clear understanding of the family unit. She is a strong woman. She can stand by herself; but now she has me, and we stand together as one. I make it a priority to put her first, even with my full schedule. I enjoy date night and use that time to reconnect and enjoy each other's company.

I feel we are alike because we both like to travel, watch good movies and plays, and read books together. In addition, we both love history and the spirit of the Lord. Some of my favorite meals Roberta prepares for me now since I am a vegan are peanut butter low-calorie smoothies, peanut butter pie, vegetable cuisine, broccoli rice, lentil beans, and sweet potato soufflé.

Although we have many similarities, we have a few differences. I like to stay up late, and she likes to go to bed early. She loves to watch certain TV programs and I like to read and listen to quiet music. These differences are minor, and come with the journey of being married. She has ways that make me laugh. She should have been a drill sergeant in the military. When she makes her bed, a nickel will bounce two feet high off it. She is a perfectionist. All my clothes must be lined up perfectly. All my undergarments, t-shirts, and socks must be "dress right dress." This is military for lined up and in perfect order. Bathroom towels must be lined up perfectly, or they are patted until they are straight. When it comes to the laundry, I will call her, tease her, and ask her how many cups of bleach to put in the colored clothes. That drives her into a panic.

Roberta supports me in my ministry in various ways. She tithes and serves as the assistant recording financial secretary of the building fund. She teaches Sunday school, and she is a part of all the women's groups, such as Women of Joy and Triumphant Women. In addition, she builds great personal relationships with the congregation members, helps in all the ministries and visits sick members. This is only a few ways she supports the ministry. The list is much longer. Moreover, she supports me in my medical practice by giving positive referrals, as well as being a great supporter in all areas of my professional life. An added bonus is that she is a great financial partner; she is a great bookkeeper and in-house accountant. I can honestly say Roberta is unique, and I cannot name anyone like her. Roberta and I share a great friendship and warm companionship.

The hardest thing I had to give up when I married Roberta was my bachelor life. However, the love we share and have received by our blended families with open arms is worth it all. She made a hard decision a no-brainer. Since we have been married, I realized that God sent her into my life for a good reason. First, the Bible reminds us that when a man finds a wife, he finds a good thing and will have favor with the Lord. (Proverbs 18:22, KJV) I have found these words to be true. She is a woman of integrity. Without a doubt, she is generous, charming, elegant, and beautiful.

Roberta is a joy to converse with on an intellectual level on one of my favorite subjects, history. Since she has taken the mantle as a senior class Sunday school teacher, she has excelled in her biblical knowledge and spiritual growth. She is a proud first lady of Church of Hope Ministries and serves with distinction in every role she is involved with in the community. She is the link of my life to the world through the gospel and the word of God. I want to thank you, Roberta, for allowing God to use you in my life, the ministry, and the united families that we are a part of.

It may seem we have a perfect relationship; my previous marriages have taught me to make adjustment. I believe I know her strengths and weaknesses, I support her in each area. It is an ongoing learning process. I am determined to not allow the mistakes I made in my past relationships tear us apart. My marriage is my top priority, as it should be. I learned that I must be in agreement with my wife. Without a doubt, this is my final love.

Frazier Sr., and third wife Roberta on their wedding day September 15, 2004

Frazier Sr., and children. Left to right: Angela, Frazier Sr., Sandra, Emmanuel, Ado, Frazier Jr., and Tobi Atlanta, GA.

Frazier Sr., son-and-daughter in law (through marriage).
Dr. Joseph Williams, wife Lynette baby Skylar.

Frazier Sr., family. Left to right: Dr. Jasper Williams III, wife Alicia, children: Jordan A, Jasper IV, Roberta Todd and Dr. Joseph Williams.

Frazier Sr., family gathering. Left to right: Noah, Angelyca, Tobi, Angela Dr. Frazier Todd, Sr., Sandra, Ado, Emmanuel and Robert, Atlanta, GA 2018

Frazier Sr., and wife Roberta, Atlanta, GA.

Frazier Sr., and wife Roberta, Atlanta, GA (2017).

Frazier Sr., with wife Roberta, Atlanta, GA (2018).

Frazier Sr., wife Roberta with daughters Angela (far left) and Sandra (front) Atlanta, GA 2016

CHAPTER 18
PODIATRIC SURGEON

Private Practice

My life as a professional podiatrist in private practice has been rewarding. I have had the opportunity to meet many outstanding professionals in the medical field and other professions. I have met judges, lawyers, ministers, civil rights workers, business CEOs, and others from the general population, all of whom had some podiatric problems, foot, or leg pain. I have treated many civil rights activists without cost because it was important to keep them walking.

The First African American – Fully Licensed
Foot and Ankle Surgical Center

I have been in the field of medicine from 1961 to the time of this writing (2018). I graduated from medical school in 1972. In 1973, I started my practice as Dr. Todd and Associates in Atlanta. In 1985, I became the first African-American podiatry physician in Georgia to operate a fully licensed foot and ankle surgical center. The name of the center was the Southwest Atlanta Foot and Ankle Surgical Center, located on Stone Hogan Road. I had a comprehensive home development business venture and have been working as a medical doctor and consultant for Southside Medical Center for over 41 years.

Second African American Podiatrist in Georgia

In the early seventies, I was the second African-American podiatrist in all of Georgia. The other podiatrist, the late Dr. Delgado, did not stay around, because he was always in Europe. He and I worked together. He would send his patients that had needed operations to my office for follow up treatment. Before long, Dr. Delgado and I had become great friends.

Dr. Delgado and I worked together on many goals in Georgia. We decided we wanted more black physicians in our specialty. Since there were only two black podiatrists practicing in the state of Georgia, we both were in great demand. Dr. Delgado and I decided to organize a recruitment plan to bring more African-American podiatric surgeons to the state of Georgia. We were successful; however, it took more than twenty years to fulfill our goals.

The first phase was to set up an approved residency surgical program at the Physicians and Surgeons Hospital off Bolton Road in Atlanta. Through this residency program, we were able to train more than thirty podiatric physicians, of which 60 percent were minorities, including females. Many of the residents remained in Georgia for their professional practices. We were able to direct several to other major cities within Georgia for their practices.

Now there are more than 50 black foot and ankle surgeons in the Georgia area, including my son, Dr. Tobi Todd. That is an impressive feeling to know that I played a part in encouraging other black men and women to succeed in my choice of profession.

In 1973, I decided to return to Atlanta for private practice. I returned to my birth hometown of Atlanta and spoke to my youngest brother, Larry, and told him, "Find me a place to practice and set it up." I did not have a place to begin my practice and did not have much capital to start it up. I sent all the legal structure papers and moved back to Atlanta to set up a practice. I only had $1,500 in savings at the bank. I had a wife (Terumi) and four kids. At the time my wife, Terumi was pregnant (with Tobi), and we had a house in California that had not sold. We were moving out of San Francisco with less than $2,000 in savings. I stepped out on faith. I was leaving a secure and comfortable job for the unknown. I knew that I would succeed, but there were so many unknown variables. I had the ability and the courage to start this venture, but God blessed me more than I could appreciate at the time.

Terumi and I packed up and I bought a new yellow-and-black car for our trip, on credit. It made it all the way to Atlanta. There were no problems. The night we drove in, Mom was happy to see us. Everybody ran out to welcome us.

After our return (Terumi and the children and I) to Atlanta in 1973, we visited the new office park on the Stone Hogan Road Connector. I saw this big, old building and was amazed. In San Francisco, I had a small office because there was not much land available.

Larry, my brother, said, "Get this whole thing, man."

I said, "It is eighteen hundred bucks a month. I cannot afford that. I don't even have a job."

He said, "You're going to need it after a while."

I agreed, and leased the entire space. The space was 1,800 square feet of office space. I did not have any medical equipment or furniture to go in it. My family helped me purchase these supplies while waiting for the office to be built as a surgical center.

It took some time for the leasing agent to build the office to my specifications, but it was all worth it.

I called my bank in California, which later became Nations Bank, which is now Bank of America; they said they could not collaborate with me living in Georgia at that time. However, my banker in California did give me an excellent reference. So, I wrote to C&S Bank (Citizen and Southern) in Georgia for a business plan loan and a line of credit.

All I was asking for was $50,000 and a line of credit to open my private practice in podiatric medicine and surgery. The banker in Georgia was reluctant to see a black person asking for a loan of this amount. My banker in California said, "Dr. Todd is a great guy and we have had this account for several years. If you don't give him a loan, I will find a banker who will." The banker at C&S told me he would approve the loan.

I was so happy. I ordered my supplies—chairs, office furniture, and other necessities. I spent about thirty thousand dollars on my office needs at that time.

Suddenly, patients just started showing up. It was interesting. While my staff was decorating my office, patients would just show up and I would take them to the emergency room. I had arranged with the local hospital emergency unit to allow me to conduct patient care in one of their rooms until my office was completed. I had nowhere else to treat them. A person would come to my office as a walk in; I would prescribe a form of treatment and say, "Come back and see me for follow up care."

Late in 1973, the builders completed my office after about six weeks, and there was a big celebration. Many of the first patients that came to my office for treatment came back to see me. At times, my family members sat in the waiting room to give the impression that they were patients and that my office was extremely busy.

In the beginning, I saw five or ten patients a day, but my family would be sitting there waiting and reading a book. After about three months, I was constantly busy. It was wonderful!

Early one Saturday morning, with a full waiting room of patients, one of my patients had made an appointment for his mother. She was from the deep southern part of South Georgia. She was white. I went to the door of the waiting room and informed the patients that I was running behind schedule because of the many emergency room referrals that morning. She shouted, "Son, you didn't tell me he was a black doctor!" The son was embarrassed. When she came into the treatment room, she was reluctant for me to examine and treat her. After the therapy had been completed, she became a regular patient and referred many of her deep southern white neighbors to the practice. This was a very humbling experience for me. She had initially rejected me because of my race, but I was accepted because of my professionalism. My conduct was able to change her negative bias against me. It is possible to have the power to change negative first impressions into lasting positive ones.

Around 1979, I remember receiving a call from a small hospital located in Franklin, Georgia, that wanted to give me an interview for employment. This was a twenty-eight-bed facility in this small town that is sixty-five miles south of Atlanta. I drove down on a Wednesday for the interview in my 1979 Cadillac with Terumi and the kids to evaluate the facility and meet the staff. I asked the hospital administrator, "Did you realize that I was a black man?"

He replied, "That's why we called you. We heard of your reputation and we need a surgical podiatrist to perform all of the foot and ankle surgery in our hospital from this community." At a loss for words, I was ecstatic. I had so many surgeries that needed to be done in my own practice. I had to collaborate with a partner, a white podiatrist, who went each week to this small hospital and performed procedures. We did this for five years until the Atlanta practice demand was too heavy for me to take a full day out of the office.

Staying Focused

I learned much about life in my years as I prepared for my future goals. At times, some incidents may have delayed my upward mobility, but I did not give up. In the military, my superior officer exposed me to bias. However, it did not stop my dreams. If anything, it may have caused a delay, but it was a learning experience, to never give up. If I felt a foot on my back, I crawled until I could stand again. Not everything I planned happened according to when I expected it to. However, I stayed focused, kept my mind clear and open, and continued to prepare and study. I have matured from these experiences. I have learned over the years not to allow my past to determine my present walk in life, nor allow it to dictate my future.

I do not allow my past choices to define where I am going tomorrow. Oftentimes, I may not have been aware of God's divine plans for me and my future. However, when I stayed focused and followed my dreams, I realized that I was blessed beyond my wildest expectations.

Army Physician and Private Practice Physician (Simultaneously)

While serving at the United States Army Hospital at Fort McPherson, Georgia, as a consultant civilian podiatrist per the Surgeon General's request, I was able to keep my connection with the Army while in private practice. After all, the Army paid for my tuition for medical school, so the least I could do was continue to serve in whatever way I could. I did not have expensive student loans.

This simultaneous civilian / Army doctoring happened around 1985 or 1986. While I was already set up in private practice, one of the Army officers, a recruiter, asked me if I wanted to come back into the Army Reserve. He informed me that I did not need weekend training. He indicated to me, "We have a new special program called IMA, (Individual Mobilization Augmentation). You would just report when you are called on active duty. Every year you must do two weeks of active duty and get your training in. Serving here at Fort McPherson will serve as part of your retirement time." I was doing it anyway, so I told him I would think about it. Before I knew it, he was at my office with my son, Frazier Jr., (who was around 29 years old) taking all my information off the wall, making copies. At that time Frazier Jr. was the manager at my practice.

A couple weeks later, I received a call from the Surgeon General's office in Washington, DC. He said, "Dr. Todd, I reviewed your application. What rank would you take?" I told him that I wanted to be a general. We both laughed. He said, "Well, if you had applied a year earlier, I could have commissioned you in a higher pay grade, as major. However, I am able to bring you no higher than a captain at this time. Would you accept that?"

I said, "Of course."

My brother Larry and I went out to Fort McPherson and I was sworn in. I was then a part of the Army Reserve and I received orders a few weeks later to report to Fort Sam Houston in San Antonio, Texas, for basic officer training, which I loved.

I also attended the Advanced Officer Class Academy in Atlanta for reserve officer training. Every summer, I would go away for two weeks to Brook Army Medical Center in San Antonio, Texas, the Military Medical Command. In addition, I had to report to Fort Stewart, Georgia, for my permanent duty station two weeks out of the year. It was a great career for me. I enjoyed it. It was like going on vacation. It can be overwhelming when you have a busy practice. I had five other physicians working for the Foot and Ankle Surgical Center. We had a full-fledged surgical center. It was a huge practice.

Once a year, I had to go on active duty to complete military training. Compared to my private practice the military hospital felt like two weeks of rest. While in my private practice, I was on call every day. However, in the military, I had only one day a week when I had to cover emergency room calls. I did not have to worry about billing insurance, filling out claims, overhead expenses, and so forth.

It was a fun and relaxing two weeks when I reported for military duty. I reported on Monday mornings. I had to go to the emergency room and cover all lower extremity injuries. That time in my life was a fun time, especially in the emergency room. The first two weeks of active duty, I remember well. My family (Terumi and the children) and I would take that period and use it as a vacation because in the last few days, I would go on active duty in December. I planned it that way because around the Christmas holidays, the Army's usual full day at the active duty stations was reduced to two days before and after Christmas. My family and I would take a trip, go to Florida from Fort Stewart, drive around there, and explore new areas. Then we would drive back to Atlanta and get ready for New Year's, as we had many times before. While that was going on, I was also called into the ministry. I did all those things by the mercy and grace of God.

Family Helping in the Business

In the 1980s my brothers, sisters, and other relatives helped me in many of my business ventures. My brother Larry operated the Church of Hope Ministries, Christian Academy Outreach Education Center, which was a dynamic program. My sister Thelma worked as an office manager, and my sister Mattie Jean was a medical assistant in my private practice. Carolyn, my baby sister, was a medical transcriptionist.

My sisters Ruth and Joan worked as teacher assistants at Church of Hope Christian Academy. They did great work. Each of my sons worked at the office every summer. My daughters Sandra and Angela would visit from San Francisco and work every summer for the practice. They lived in California with their mother, Nancy. I had learned how to do something I saw practiced in other communities: keeping the business in the family so the family would be blessed by the family's efforts.

My Dream Tumbles Down

The family is the building block of the community. If you have strong families, your community is strong. Because the medical complex was successful, I reached out for another goal. This was to purchase 175 acres of land and build a new first-timer's home development on one hundred acres. This was to include a comprehensive church community center with a drug rehabilitation program and an academic center for the community. This would allow the community to make progressive life improvements within the area.

My dream came tumbling down after the housing market crash that set off the 1981 to 1982 recession. I lost all my cash investment of more than $1.5 million. I felt deep pain, but not devastation. It was like a blow to my stomach that knocked me down but I got up. I knew I would recover. This was a temporary setback.

In spite of these losses, God stepped in and gave me another blessing in an investment that I was not fully aware of. My portfolio included an investment in minerals in Africa. My family (Terumi and kids) and I were still able to maintain our middle-class lifestyle.

Finding a Home to Practice Medicine in the Community

I became part of the staff of Southside Medical Center (SMC) in Atlanta, in 1976, I few years after I began my private podiatric medical practice. I am honored to call SMC "home" for the last forty-two years.

SMC is a multiple disciplinary medical center that originated out of the heart of one registered nurse, Mrs. Lucille Hill, and others in 1965. It began with a humble mission: to take care of the medically underserved within the south Atlanta communities. Fifty-plus years later, SMC serves thousands of underserved residents throughout the state of Georgia. SMC currently operates nine centers, including two housing units that house families that are HIV positive.

In the early 1970s, Dr. Lee Shelton (SMC board member) called my office and said that the center needed a dependable podiatric surgeon to help take care of their patients. He offered me the position. I also had an offer from Grady Memorial Health System. I had to make a decision between SMC and Grady Memorial Health System. I chose SMC.

I worked at SMC one half-day per week until my retirement from private practice in 2005/2006. From my retirement time my hours increased and I began serving fulltime as the director of the Specialty Department. This department has the responsibility for all cardiology, general surgery, peripheral vascular disease, infectious disease, podiatric/wound care, and the evening and weekend clinics. I was promoted to director of this department because of my experience and hard work.

My military experience helped to groom and mature me to serve in this capacity. I am honored to be a part of this community and serve to help complete the multiple missions and tasks as medical ambassador to the different communities.

I want to thank the president/CEO, Dr. David Williams of SMC, for giving me this opportunity to repay my city and community with the skills I have learned over the years. It is an honor.

Frazier Sr., at the medical office around 1973, smiling with patient, Atlanta, GA

Dr. Todd and Associates, Foot and Ankle Surgery office, 1st opening 1973 in Atlanta, GA.

FRAZIER "BEN" TODD, SR., D. P. M.
ANNOUNCES THE OPENING OF AN OFFICE
FOR THE PRACTICE OF
PODIATRY (FOOT SPECIALIST)
FOR CHILDREN AND ADULTS
SUITE 310 — EXECUTIVE PARK SOUTH
2945 STONE HOGAN ROAD CONNECTOR, S. W.
ATLANTA, GEORGIA 30331

OFFICE HOURS:
BY APPOINTMENT

TELEPHONE:
349-5100

Dr. Frazier Todd, Sr. and son, Dr. Tobi Todd with patient, Atlanta, GA, 2004.

Frazier Sr., with older patient, Atlanta, GA

Dr. Frazier B. Todd, Sr., with great grandchildren (left to right) Dayana and Dylan at Southside Medical Center.

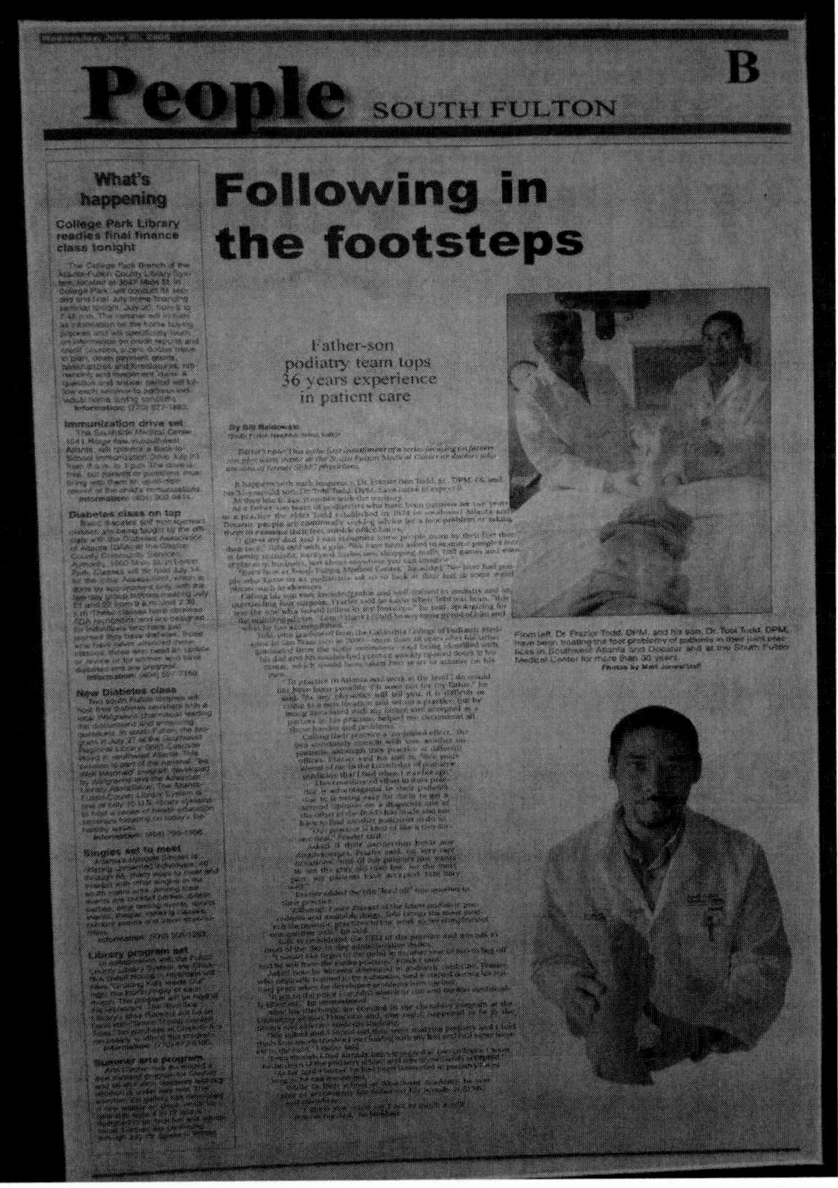

People B

SOUTH FULTON

What's happening

College Park Library readies final finance class tonight

Immunization drive set

Diabetes class on tap

New Diabetes class

Singles set to meet

Library program set

Summer arts program

Following in the footsteps

Father-son podiatry team tops 36 years experience in patient care

Dr. Frazier B. Todd, Sr., and son Dr. Tobi Todd featured in South Fulton (Atlanta) newspaper article July 20, 2005.

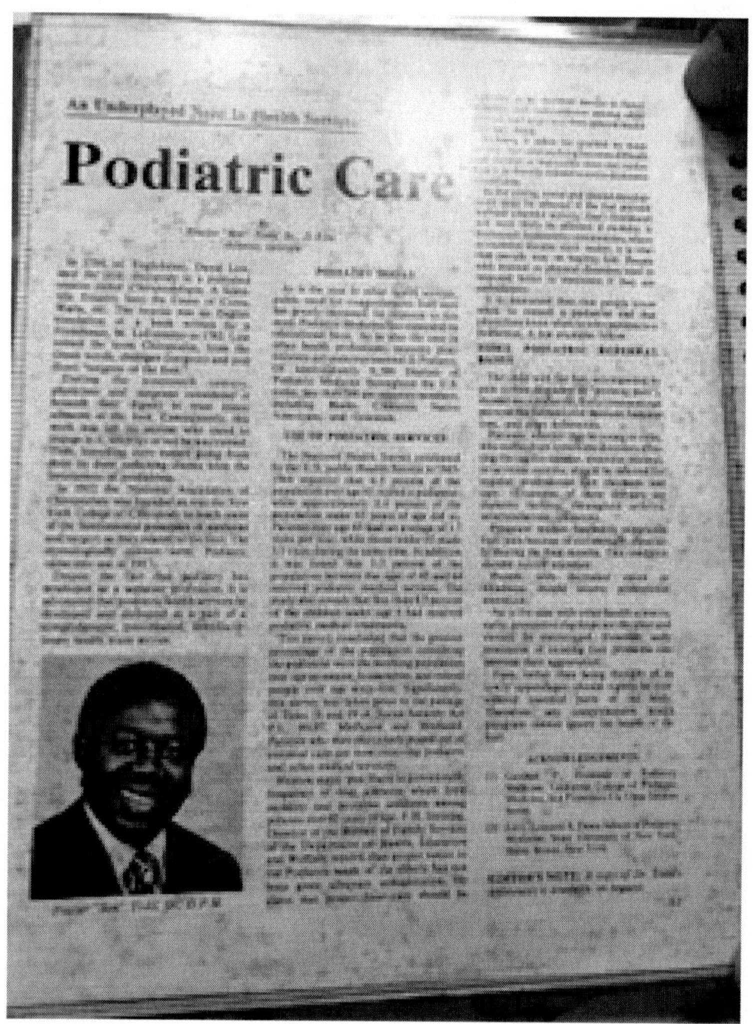

An Underplayed Need In Health Services

Podiatric Care

Frazier, Sr., news article - joining the staff at Heard County Memorial Hospital, Georgia.

ATLANTA DAILY WORLD Sunday April 21, 1974

Dr. Todd Returns Home To Help Correct Local Foot Problems

DR. FRAZIER BEN TODD

Dr. Fraizer Ben Todd, who grew up in Southeast Altanta, completing elementary school at Thomasville Elementary School, has returned home as one of Georgia's two black podiatrists (foot specialists).

A graduate of Morehouse College, Dr. Todd completed in pre-medical studies at the University of San Francisco. He graduated from the California College of Podiatric Medicine and did his internship and surgical residency at the California Podiatric Medical Center.

Before returning to Atlanta, Dr. Todd served as assistant professor of Podiatric Medicine, Surgery and Biomechanics at the medical center.

In an effort to meet the need for podiatrist here, Dr. Todd has opened offices at Executive Park South, 2945 Stone Hogan Rd. Connector, SW in Suite 10.

He attended David T. Howard High and was a member of the famous Blue & Gold Marching Band. He was transferred to L.J. Price High where he was one of the leading trumpet soloist. His most famous musical debut was when he appeared in the Atlanta Symphony young people's concert as guest soloist, playing the last movements of Haydns Trumpet Concert in B-flat.

Frazier Sr., returns home to Atlanta, to open medical office, 1974.

CHAPTER 19
A TIME TO SHARE

Charities

Growing up, my older siblings would give and share their belongings with younger family members. The older brother or sister would pass on their clothing to the one closest in age. I saw and learned this way of giving through my parents, as they taught me how to care and share.

I recall a major community event when I was about eight years old living on Phillips Drive in the Thomasville community. My father, Floyd Henry Todd, had been ill and was unable to work for an extended period. One night, a convoy of cars drove up to our home and parked in the field, yard, and roadway. The people got out of their automobiles carrying large bags of groceries and other non-perishable items. Families made up this group. They filled our tables, chairs, the kitchen cabinets, even the back porch and other areas of our home, with food. Wow! The family received an impressive gift of food supply that would last our family for three months. We did not need any milk or meat, because our cow, Daisy, supplied milk, and our smokehouse was almost full of meat because the meat from the hogs had been stored there.

This episode was an early teaching moment, as I later realized how important it is to give back and plant seeds within the community you live in. My father was continually active in community affairs. He was an officer of Mount Carmel AME, our family church. He was also an active member of the local Masonic Lodge. I learned from the seed planted in my heart and from other experiences that I have a duty to share and give in the place of my heritage. I also came to understand that "no man is an island," and that "no man stands alone." We are all interconnected, to be there to pick up a falling brother or sister. It was from these humble beginnings that I, too, like my father and older siblings, picked up the mantle and gave back.

I began that process of giving back at an early age by becoming a Cub Scout, later a Boy Scout, and was actively involved in the youth department in our church, especially in the music department. I remember many other areas of involvement working with other youths from our community and high school. These activities helped to develop my character.

Years later, after joining the Army, the military solidified my compassion by teaching the basic principles that I am my brother's keeper. He or she watches your back while you watch his or her back. My youth and military experience led me to be more active as an adult community member.

I recall an older man who reminded me of my father when I was a pre-medical student in San Francisco. This man loved baseball and did not have anyone to take him to see the Giants play at Candlestick Park. I made it my mission to pick him up on many occasions, when I was available, to take him to see his favorite baseball team.

I have also learned that it is not right to just place my name on a role of an organization. I must have an active part within the structure and purpose of that organization. I need to be actively involved. For example, I worked diligently with the National Association for the Advancement of Colored People (NAACP) during the crisis of the missing children in Atlanta in 1979–1981. I served as the chairperson of the church committee to arrange for prayer groups in multiple churches of all faiths so that the perpetrator of Atlanta's missing, and murdered children would be found. I tried to do something specific in the organizations I support.

Here is a list of some organizations that I am a member of and/or support. These organizations, and others like them, do wonderful things for people in need, for communities, youth, and health.

1. AARP (American Association of Retired Persons)
2. Feeding America
3. NMAAHC (National Museum of African American History and Culture)
4. AFPCC (American Federation of Police and Concerned Citizens)
5. ACS (American Cancer Society)
6. American Lung Society
7. American Diabetes Society
8. American Podiatric Medical Association
9. NAACP (National Association for the Advancement of Colored People)
10. Schomburg Center for Research in Black Culture
11. Southern Poverty High Museum Center
12. High Museum of Art and more.

CHAPTER 20
MY FAITH

What I Believe to be True

My faith began as a young child, watching my parents pray and gather the family around for all special occasions. In the morning, we had a prayer at breakfast, and then again, every night before we went to bed. My parents had a house full of children, and I had to pay attention to the prayers and the direction our parents gave us. Later, at Sunday school at the home church, Mt. Carmel AME, I learned about Bible characters, especially my favorite character, Daniel, and the experiences of Shadrach, Meshach, and Abednego. I learned how to remember their names by shaking the bed, making the bed, and to bed, we go.

These experiences started my quest for the search for truth in my faith walk; through the example of my parents' faith, and later as I became a member in the congregation and I would listen to the pastor. We had church all day on Sunday, starting with Sunday school, the morning service, then we would have playtime. However, we would go back in the evening at six o'clock and then have the night service. This all kept us busy. We did not have a television at that time. In the forties and fifties, they were not available in our community.

Other favorite characters in the Bible are Abraham, Moses, Paul and Peter. I learned from the life of Abraham that sometimes in life, I must make changes, and when I make those changes by traveling to a different place, many more doors will open as I have experienced in both my military and civilian life.

I learned from Moses that I will have some wilderness experiences, but those experiences will allow me to grow and mature and learn how to overcome difficult situations easier and with more confidence had I not had that wilderness experience.

I learned from the life of Paul that I must listen and make a change in my direction and in my life.

I learned from Peter, the rock, the foundation that stood for something that Christ saw in him. Peter recognized the rock in Christ himself, and he was an imitator of the rock. Therefore, I know I must be a rock for my family and a rock for the community so that they can see me as a stabilizing force, as Peter saw Christ.

To sum it all up, my faith is still in the growing stage. I am at the infant stage; I am not mature all the way. Nevertheless, I am working toward the maturation process. It took Moses forty years in the wilderness. I do not know how long it is going to take me, but I am learning more each day as I grow in my faith. "Faith is the substance of things hoped for" (Hebrews 11:1). It is the evidence of things I know I am going to see. I have already seen God's power and action in my life and the lives of my family members.

As a senior pastor of the Church of Hope Ministries at Perkerson, I am actively involved in restorative justice practices (a social movement, philosophy and a set of practices) that has been around in North America for over 40 years. However, restorative practices is not new it has been around since the creation of man. For biblically, God is the creator of justice in the form of the fruits of the spirits. The mission of the Church of Hope Ministries at Perkerson is to be a family of Christians who believe in helping others. Our vision is to be proficient in ministry and active in outreach programs. Our goals are training, collaboration, strategic participation, structure leadership, research/funding, prayer, and restorative practices. The COHM at Perkerson had fourteen leaders of the church to go through a six month training in restorative church conflict management. This training ended in a cap and gown graduation. The graduates were from various academic backgrounds from doctoral degrees to non - high school diplomas. The leaders were from age thirty-four to seventy-two. COHM has used restorative dialog for challenging conflict among members, as community building and as healing circles during the death of a youth and another youth wounded from gun violence. The restorative justice ministry is under the leadership of Minister Janice Jerome, an outstanding leader in this field. She was appointed in 2016 as one of the leaders in restorative justice for the University of Texas at Austin.

Janice also developed the shoebox ministry, which is a special ministry for the youth of the community who receives gifts in a box at Christmas time. This ministry allows the many young people to receive school supplies, toys, clothing, and other items during the Christmas holiday season.

Dr. Frazier Ben Todd, Sr., Pastor of Church of Hope Ministries at Perkerson, 2018, Atlanta, GA

Church of Hope and Perkerson Baptist Church Restorative class leaders. Left to right, Janice Jerome, Roberta Todd, Samuel Brooks, Iesha Brooks, Debora Conklin. Back row, Dr. Frazier B. Todd, Sr., John Manelos, Devadas Lynton Atlanta, GA 2014

2014 Restorative Justice Graduation. Left to right: Roberta Todd, Dr. Frazier B. Todd, Sr., Pastor and granddaughter Denaya, Atlanta, GA

Frazier Sr., with family singing at Church of Hope Ministries. Left to right: Frazier Sr., Tobi, Ado, Emmanuel and Terumi. (1993)

CHAPTER 21
THE JOURNEY HOME

Atlanta, Georgia

In 1962, I was married to my first wife, Nancy, and living in California when I was transferred to central Korea. I brought the family back to Atlanta to live with Nancy's grandmother. We had a special room built for her in the house. I had one of my father's friends, Deacon White, build that room in the house within a two-week period. He was a licensed carpenter who used to do work with my Dad. He and my dad were deacons at their respective churches. That was where my family stayed when I deployed to Korea.

At that point in my life, I had never been overseas to live, and I was going to be stationed in Korea for thirteen months. My company and I traveled by ship, it looked like a World War II troop carrier. Soldiers were throwing up! It was a miserable trip, but I volunteered to work in the hospital on the troop carrier ship USNS *Gaffey* because I was a medical technologist, able to work in the lab and support the medical crew.

The USNS *Gaffey* crew was looking for a musician to organize a band. I thought to myself, I could do that. I put a call out for all the musicians. I played the piano and the trumpet. I organized a band of about sixteen people. We were called the

Moon River Band because that is the one song, we played that everybody loved. "Moon River" written by Johnny Mercer and made popular by Frank Sinatra. The band and I practiced every day for about two hours. I was the leader, so I would write out the music and give out the parts. The unit really wanted to come up and get out of the hole at the bottom of the ship.

When we crossed the International Dateline, the band had to play that night. We had a big party. We had five good songs that we had learned how to play and we played them repeatedly. We played them as long as we could. We were really jamming! That was a fun party.

When the shipped arrived in Korea, the smell of the atmosphere was not pleasant. I had never smelled a smell like that. When we landed in Inchon, the Navy came out and picked us up with a land barge that we could not walk on, so they put us on a raft and took us in one hundred or two hundred at a time. There were about five thousand troops on the ship.

Following the United Nations plan, we had to rotate one for one; one military personnel (based upon the occupation specialty) would replace other military personnel.

If they needed a mechanic over there, they sent a mechanic; if they needed a cook, they sent a cook to replace the cook who was rotating out. When I checked in and signed in according to Army protocol, the soldier I was replacing came to meet me. I got there at least two weeks before the soldier left so I could become familiar with his job. The soldier was so happy to see me because he could not leave until I arrived.

Once I found my quarters where I would live; it was very pleasant.

The next day after I had checked into the post with my military credentials and arrived at the dispensary where I would work, I met a native Korean, Mr. Song Song Oh. He was about four feet tall; he was the civilian medical technologist working for the department of the Army. He bowed to me with his head almost touching the floor and asked me my name. He saw it on my lapel: Todd. He asked me, "Where are you from?" I told him Atlanta, Georgia. He took a piece of paper and drew an outline of the United States of America, then he drew the shape of the state of Georgia on the southeast corner, then he drew a circle where Atlanta was and said, "This is your home." I was impressed because while I knew where I lived, I was not capable of drawing that geographical demonstration of my home, nor could I draw his country in that manner. Remember, math was my strong suit in school, not geography.

We also had a Katsu; a Korean soldier. I trained him as a medical laboratory specialist. In addition, that was how we worked together; the civilian, the American soldier, and the Korean soldier, working at the same job at the hospital.

Highest Alert (Cuban Missile Crisis in South Korea)

The Army's highest alert happened in Korea during the Cuban Missile Crisis of 1962, issued weapons and everything, for the inevitable. The United States Army was preparing for the North Koreans to cross the demilitarized zone (DMZ). My unit was genuinely concerned. I remember having a special ID, other than my military ID, to perform certain duties in the event that happened. I was the chemical biological warfare specialist in my unit. I cannot elaborate further without violating any military codes. I will never forget that time in Korea during the Cuban Missile Crisis in 1962. Then, it seemed just as quickly as it started, it was over.

My Family Joins me in Korea

My family, Nancy and the children; Frazier Jr., Sandra, and Angela were especially important to me. I missed them very much so I made special arrangements for them to join me in Korea. The Army did not cover the relocation expenses of my family. They came over on a civilian air flight. I arranged for them to live in Seoul, Korea, at the United Nations village, and I could visit with them weekly, on the weekends. That was a blessing to me because my family was critical to me.

Never made it to Kentucky

After completing my military assignment in Korea in 1963, my family and I returned to the United States. The Army's plane arrived at Travis Air Force Base in California. Once I stepped off the plane I kissed the ground because I was so glad to be back in America with my family. It had been over a year since I had been in the United States. To my surprise the family stay in California would be short lived.

My new assignment was in Fort Knox, Kentucky. I bought a station wagon (a roomy car) for the family, and we were on our way to Fort Knox, Kentucky. During our travel to Fort Knox, I stopped and used a pay phone to call Mom. While on the phone Mom told me, "Son, you have to go back to California." I asked her why. She said, "We have a telegram here for you. Go back to California; the Army is going to send you to the school out there in California rather than Texas." I was surprised and happy to receive the message from Mom however, I continued to travel home to Atlanta and visited with my mother and family. The family and I never made it to Kentucky.

That is how God worked it out for me to get back to California. Atlanta was the home for Fort McPherson Armed Forces Command Headquarter (FORSCOM); this is where I was able to pick up my once-a-month regular paycheck. During this time, there were no electronic ways to receive a paycheck. After about 30 days of being in Atlanta, I went back to San Francisco, California, in preparation for school.

For fifty-two weeks, I was at the Letterman General Hospital for the Advanced Medical Technology Military Medical School. I reported to Letterman Hospital US Army Command in San Francisco. The US Army Command placed me in the medical lab because of my past training and experience. At that point, before I became a residence student in the advanced class, I worked in different departments for three months. In this role, I was able to meet many of my future professors and instructors.

That advanced class ran for fifty-two weeks, eight hours a day. When I finished that class, it was the equivalent to a master's degree in basic science. I was so happy when I finished that class. It was a new beginning.

Several of the class members received their commissions for the military. I was still non-commissioned because I had not yet received my official Bachelor of Science degree. However, I did get that basic science degree, and they taught me well. Later, when I went to medical school, (because of all the military training) I had an equivalent to a master's degree.

I finished that class and because of my certification process, I could work part-time in California in the medical laboratory field. I did that in a Presbyterian hospital. Everything paid off. I had some excellent friends in the best environment in the Bay area. I was able to finish my college undergrad and get my degree. I went to San Francisco State University and all the while, I was in active duty in the Army.

I had a scholarship to medical school in Kansas and a scholarship in California. However, I did not have a scholarship for the California College of Podiatric Medicine (Samuel Merritt University), which was where I wanted to go. It was more convenient for me there; I did not want to move. So, the GI bill (Government Issue Bill for Veterans) took care of my expense.

I was a medical technology student in the Army at Letterman General Hospital when President Kennedy was assassinated in 1963. I remember those events very clearly. I was out on the floor, collecting specimens for the lab, when I noticed that many doctors and other staff were crying as they stood around the telegraph machine. "What's going on?" I asked.

One doctor was saying aloud, "The president, the president." Then he turned to me and said, "President Kennedy is dead." He was truly angry and sad.

That was a crushing blow to me. I went back to the lab and told everyone that President Kennedy had been assassinated. Everyone stood there in shock. It was a shock to us all as Americans, and especially at the military post.

When I arrived home that night, Nancy had been crying. She was devastated. San Francisco became a city of sadness and gloom. It looked like the world had come to a standstill at that moment because of the many people who loved President Kennedy. I am sure there were some people who did not care for him, but it was something to behold to see America at that moment. I will never forget that time. Tears come to my eyes now when I think about it. A dark cloud had descended upon America.

I remembered how less than a year earlier, when I was in Korea, President Kennedy had put the nation on high alert. The U.S. was dealing with the Cuban Missile Crisis, just waiting for the blockade around Cuba, and now the president was gone.

Vietnam Theater of Operations Lessons

While serving in the Vietnam theater of operations as discussed previously, we would leave every Monday and come back on Thursday. Many of my friends did not come back, but I did. It was a great learning experience I will never forget. It was in the military that I became a man—a real man.

I learned how to manage things, how to take responsibility, how not to make excuses, how to stand up and be a man and do what I needed to do to take care of the situation at that moment. My military career was one of the most rewarding of its kind in the whole world.

As I look back on my nine years in active duty—Vietnam, the issues I had in the military, the battles I had to fight as a black man—I felt equal opportunity was more prevalent in the military than anywhere else in America.

I remember those difficult times during the civil rights movement when Dr. Martin Luther King, Jr. was marching. I was a supporter, but a silent supporter, because in the military, black men could not do certain things. Even though I was a US Citizen I could not be a Democrat, Republican, or Independent. I could not acknowledge any alliance. I had to be apolitical.

I do not know how I figured out my life path, but everything just directed me back home. I remember on many earlier visits to Atlanta, Mom asked, "Are you coming back to Atlanta?"

I said, "No, Mom. I'm never coming back there." Each time I came back to Atlanta to visit, everything looked better; pleasant and more progressive.

Before I left Atlanta in 1958, the civil government was all non-black. However, the black community in Atlanta was expanding. The black community was no longer "the black community"; it was *the* community. Public parks, (closed due to segregation when I was a child), were now opened to blacks, and blacks were living all over Atlanta. I saw the homes and the possibilities . . . but I loved the San Francisco Bay area. It was becoming difficult to make a decision to stay in California or move back to Atlanta. When Nancy and I were married I was happy living in California. However, by the time I married Terumi in 1967, the possibility of moving to Atlanta became attractive. There was one incident in 1972 that broke the camel's back; it was the last straw that helped me decide. I took my children and my current wife Terumi, who was pregnant with our son Tobi, to a Giants baseball game at Candlestick Park.

We drove to the front parking area. The attendant said, "Parking here is five dollars," or whatever the fee was. I saw a spot at the front gate and assumed that was where we were going to park. I paid him, but he had us follow cars to park the car much farther away from the parking area I paid for. Admissions to the game, meant we had to walk down the high hill back to the gate. I was disappointed with that experience. Later at the stadium, I bought Cokes and snacks for the children, and the Cokes had been watered down. They tasted like colored water at an expensive price. That experience made up my mind. I said, I am not going to stay in San Francisco, I am going back to Atlanta, where I think things will be much better. A Coke will taste like a Coke, because Atlanta is home of the Coca Cola factory. I missed my siblings and Mom anyway, they were constantly asking me to come home. I made up my mind in that moment. I felt cheated at that moment in San Francisco, and I would rather be home.

That Monday, I got on the telephone and called my brother Larry. I said, "Larry, find me a house in Atlanta, I am coming home." He was so happy. Mom and everybody were so thrilled that we were moving back home. I returned to Atlanta for two main reasons to start my private practice and to be with my mother, siblings, and extended family again.

Around 1973, I went down to city hall in Atlanta and there was a young, black girl working as a receptionist who greeted me. To my amazement, I saw a black woman at the front desk in city hall in Atlanta. When I left Atlanta in 1958, white people held receptionist positions in government. A black receptionist in city hall of Atlanta, Georgia; there were black folks at the state capitol, not cutting grass or sweeping floors!

Unique Black Medical Complex Open Near Greenbriar

"We're unique," says Dr. Frazier "Ben" Todd, one of only two Black podiatrists in Georgia, about the medical complex that is evolving in Executive Park South, off the Stone-Hogan Road Connector. "This may be the only all-Black complex in the country with adequate waiting room for patients. We're certainly one of the first sophisticated, sedate complexes in the South." More than that, Dr. Todd promises, those plush waiting rooms are not likely to be filled with impatiently waiting sufferers because all doctors in Executive Park South work by appointments. "The average waiting time is 20-25 minutes," Dr. Todd says.

Todd himself was just finishing up his second week of occupancy in his handsome suite of offices in Executive Park South when the VOICE visited him there. Some of his rooms are still vacant, waiting for the delivery of equipment held up by the truckers' strike, but his laboratory is fully equipped and his two ample waiting rooms are comfortably decorated. Like the other doctors in the complex, Dr. Todd is on the staff of a local hospital--the new facility on Bolton Road, in Todd's case. The doctors try to get to their Executive Park South offices in the afternoons, and some of them are still there well into the evening.

The buildings in which the complex is located were built one-and-a-half or two years ago, but the first medical facility moved in last August. This was Medical Measurements, a "paramedics facility," in the words of its head nurse, Mrs. Grace Lewis, which gives physical examinations to the employees of companies that request their services. So far, nine companies have authorized

About three or four months ago, a fully equipped pharmacy opened in the complex, partly owned by pharmacist Brady Cooper, who has long operated a drug store at West Lake and Simpson. The other pharmacist is Willie Harris, who calls the prices of his drugs, cosmetics, magazines, and soft drinks competitive with those at the nearby Super-X. The pharmacy also sells mail orders. At present it is open from 10 a.m. till 8 p.m., but pharmacist Harris anticipates that the evening hours may be extended as more doctors fill the complex.

At about the same time as the pharmacy opened, the Southwest Women's Clinic came to Executive Park South. Here gynecology and obstetrics are practiced. The Clinic's ample facilities include an education room where films are shown and exercises for natural childbirth are taught. Medical assistant Jennifer Clark showed the VOICE around and pointed proudly to the speculums heated to body temperatures as one of the Clinic's features that provides special comfort for its patients.

The complex boasts another women's facility, the Atlanta Women's Pavilion, under the administrative directorship of Mrs. Joan Toney. This abortion clinic is open for appointments from 8:30 a.m. to 4:30 p.m. and charges $150 for the operation, with the possibility of reducing or waiving the fees.

In addition, the complex contains an orthopedic surgeon, Dr. Joseph I. Hoffman, Jr.; two family physicians, Dr. Otis McCree and Dr. John Mayes; and a brand newcomer, Dr. Gerald Hood. As Dr. Todd pointed out, "almost" total health care is furnished in the complex. As of now, they are without a dentist, a pediatrician, and a dermatologist, but each of these specialists is being recruited. Dawson Realty Company, which has offices in Executive Park South, spearheaded the move to assemble a medical complex there and continues to work to expand it.

As for Dr. Todd himself, he calls his field, podiatry, "the best-kept secret in the United States," since so few Black people even know of its existence. Requirements to be licensed has as podia trist are slightly lower tha requirements for an M. I but Todd says only some 5(out of roughly 10,000 podia trists in the country a Black. Finally now, acco ding to Todd, an effort being made to recruit mo minorities into the field pc diatry, and Todd himsel actively engaged in that re cruitment process.

Frazier Sr., opens up the first fully license foot and ankle center in Greenbriar area of Atlanta.

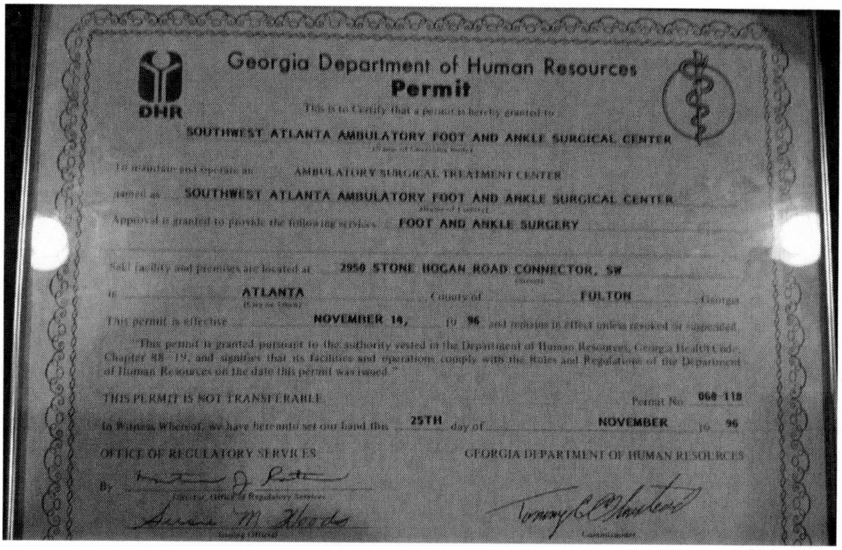

DHR

Georgia Department of Human Resources

Permit

This is to Certify that a permit is hereby granted to

SOUTHWEST ATLANTA AMBULATORY FOOT AND ANKLE SURGICAL CENTER

To maintain and operate an AMBULATORY SURGICAL TREATMENT CENTER

named as **SOUTHWEST ATLANTA AMBULATORY FOOT AND ANKLE SURGICAL CENTER**

Approval is granted to provide the following services: **FOOT AND ANKLE SURGERY**

Said facility and premises are located at **2950 STONE HOGAN ROAD CONNECTOR, SW**

in **ATLANTA** County of **FULTON** Georgia

This permit is effective **NOVEMBER 14,** 19 **96** and remains in effect unless revoked or suspended.

"This permit is granted pursuant to the authority vested in the Department of Human Resources, Georgia Health Code, Chapter 88-19, and signifies that its facilities and operations comply with the Rules and Regulations of the Department of Human Resources on the date this permit was issued."

THIS PERMIT IS NOT TRANSFERABLE. Permit No. **060 118**

In Witness Whereof, we have hereunto set our hand this **25TH** day of **NOVEMBER** 19 **96**

OFFICE OF REGULATORY SERVICES

GEORGIA DEPARTMENT OF HUMAN RESOURCES

By

Director, Office of Regulatory Services

Issuing Official

Commissioner

CHAPTER 22
BLESSED FROM THE BEGINNING

I have lived an exciting, enriched, and happy life. It has been filled with love, support, and my childhood desire to travel. I owe all the successes that I have achieved to God, my parents, my family, my friends, my classmates, my Christian community and many others including the communities of Atlanta that supported a native son in every effort I was involved. I owe a debt of gratitude to all my teachers, from the first grade in the four-room school in the community of Thomasville of southeast Atlanta to Howard High School, Price High School, Morehouse College, the military, medical school and many more that I do not have enough room to name.

I have been married three times. I had the greatest supporters of my successes in each one of my marriages. In total, my wives gave me six wonderful children whom we all love and cherish. I have learned much on how to be a better husband, and thus a better man, under the anointing of God my Creator, Jesus, my Activator, and the Holy Spirit, my Operator. It is my hope that the reader of my adventures will learn, grow, and develop a sense of confidence that life is a never-ending cycle of hope and endurance when you have God on your side.

My experiences as a son, brother, husband, father, soldier, doctor, pastor, community leader, and Christian have given me a diverse opportunity to see how God works in this world we live in. There are too many highlights for me to mention in this book. However, America, my home is one of the best countries for a black man like me to be born in; I have had many opportunities to develop into full maturity because I took advantage of the doors that were open to me. I did not focus on what appears to be a closed door. I continued to knock until one was opened. I did not give up when the first door closed in my face. I prepared to keep the oil burning by studying and being ready when that door opened. I kept on knocking, and suddenly the door that God wanted me to enter opened. I did not give up in discouragement.

I believe that my faith in God, my perseverance, and my strong-rooted family values are the reason why I was blessed from the beginning.

* * *

MESSAGE FROM THE CHILDREN OF DR. FRAZIER BEN TODD, SR.

"My father continues to make his own path. This book could never capture all his accomplishments and struggles. Nevertheless, I appreciate and love him for having the courage to share intimate portions of his life." ~Tobi Todd, DPM

"While my mother taught me patience in a world of frustration and aggravation, my father taught me that a change in my feelings and mentality is a change in my destiny. Dad, I love you, and thank you for being my father!" ~Emmanuel G. Todd

"My dad is my hero. He taught me how to be an entrepreneur. He is a man of God and he showed me how to forgive. Love you, and proud of you always." ~Frazier Ben Todd Jr.

"My dad has always been my hero because he has a heart of gold. He is always giving of himself to help or to inspire others. He is the kindest, smartest, hardworking man I know. Thank you, Daddy, for guiding me through this journey called life. Your laugh is contagious, and your smile is infectious! I love you and I am so proud of you! You did it!" ~Angela Bohannon

"My dad's laughter is something I will always remember. He always finds humor in his children. He also has insight into each of us. He is strong and steady, with a heart overflowing with love. He is the rock of this huge family, and so many depend on him. I'm immensely proud of him." ~Sandra Martin

"My father, the doctor, was a pioneer in his medical specialty field. He trained all his sons to be pioneers and entrepreneurs. I am one of the chips off the block because of his leadership. I am the president of Adorable Pools, serving as the CEO. I work with my brother Emmanuel Gabriel Todd in serving many of the recreational swimming pools in the greater Atlanta, Georgia, area." ~Ado T. Todd

BIOGRAPHY

Dr. Frazier Ben Todd Sr., DPM, CWS, DABPS, DABDA, DAAWN, DNBPE, FACFAS, has had a remarkable life and a distinguished career. He was the first African American physician in Georgia to run a fully licensed foot and ankle surgical center. He was the first African American physician to chair the Podiatric Surgical Residency program in Atlanta at the Physicians and Surgeons Hospital. Also, he was one of the first surgical residency-trained African American Podiatric surgeons in Georgia.

Frazier Ben Todd Sr. was born in Riverdale, Georgia, and raised in the Thomasville community in the city of Atlanta. After graduation in 1957 from Price Judson High School (where he holds the distinction of being the first trumpet soloist), Dr. Todd attended several undergraduate schools. He attended Morehouse College (Atlanta), San Antonio College (San Antonio, Texas), US Army Science Academy Medical Field Service School (Ft. Sam Houston, Texas), Cochise College (Arizona), San Francisco State College (California), University of San Francisco (California), and the California College of Podiatric Medicine. Dr. Todd earned his Bachelor of Science degree in Medical Science in 1969. In 1972, he earned his Doctor of Podiatric Medicine degree from the California College of Podiatric Medicine.

Dr. Todd joined the US Navy Reserve in 1956 and the US Army in 1958. While in the US Army, Dr. Todd continued his undergraduate studies at Cochise College in Arizona, San Francisco State College, and the University of San Francisco.

His post-graduate training includes a podiatric surgical residency in foot and ankle surgery, Pacific Coast Hospital (California, 1972, 1973); Fellowship, Atlanta Hospital (1984–1986); Uniformed Services University of the Health Sciences-Military Medicine Education Institute (1986, 1987, 1990); and Interdenominational Theological Center Seminary Class of 2006.

Board certifications include Fellow - American College of Foot and Ankle Surgeons; Diplomat - American Board of Podiatric Surgery; Diplomat - National Board of Podiatry Examiners; Diplomat - American Academy of Wound Management; and Senior Disability Analyst.

His employment history includes: CEO/president private practice at three different locations in Georgia (1974–2006), including a foot and ankle surgical center; CEO/medical director of southwest Atlanta Ambulatory Foot and Ankle Surgical Center (1996–2006); assistant professor and lecturer at five of the College of Podiatric Medicine and Surgery centers (California College of Podiatric Medicine, 1972–1973); supervisor at Clinical Laboratory Presbyterian Hospital, San Francisco, CA (1967–1972); primary military occupational specialty (medical lab specialist) US Army (1958–1967); residency director, surgical residency PSR24, Physicians and Surgeons Hospital, Atlanta, GA (1985–1991); major, US Army Reserve, Ft. Stewart, GA (1984); retired podiatrist, 1999; served in the theaters of operation - Vietnam and Operation Desert Storm; podiatric consultant, Southside Medical Center, Atlanta, GA (1974–current.)

Dr. Todd also worked as adjunct clinical instructor at the following medical schools (1974–2006): Barry College of Podiatric Medicine; California College of Podiatric Medicine;

Chicago College of Podiatric Medicine; Dr. William Schools College of Podiatric Medicine; Iowa College of Podiatric Medicine; Morehouse School of Medicine; New York College of Podiatric Medicine, and Ohio College of Podiatric Medicine.

Dr. Todd's hospital affiliations include (1973–2006): Atlanta Hospital and Medical Center, Columbia Northlake Medical Center (GA); Decatur Hospital (GA); Eisenhower Army Medical Center (GA); Physicians and Surgeons Hospital (GA); South Fulton Hospital and Medical Center (GA); WellStar Windy Hill (GA); Southwest Atlanta Ambulatory Foot and Ankle Surgical Center; Winn Army Hospital, Ft. Stewart, Georgia.

Dr. Todd's professional and civic organization affiliations include: American Academy of Wound Management; American Board of Disability Analysts; American Diabetes Association; American Podiatric Medical Association; American Society of Medical Technologists; Association for the Advancement of Wound Care; Georgia Podiatric Medical Association; National Podiatric Medical Association; National Rehabilitation Association, and the Neuropathy Association, Atlanta Medical Association, Georgia State Medical Association.

Having completed surgical residency training in San Francisco, Dr. Todd established his medical practice in 1973 in the southwest Atlanta Greenbriar community. To better serve his patients, he opened a second office in 1978 in the Gresham Road area, and a third office, the Wesley Chapel Foot and Ankle Center in Decatur, Georgia, in 1980. He has served as the medical director and the chief executive officer of the Southwest Atlanta Ambulatory Foot and Ankle Center.

His civic associations include: Alpha Gamma Kappa Fraternity; Atlanta Chamber of Commerce; Master Mason,

Shriner 32nd degree; Millennium Financial Service-Planning Development, Inc.; the National Association for the Advancement of Colored People (NAACP). He has collaborated with the Boys Scouts of America, the Girl Scouts of America, the Boys and Girls Club, the Little League Association, the Parent Teacher Association, the Southwest Atlanta Community Association, and the East Point Clean Community Association.

Dr. Todd is an accomplished speaker and lecturer for medical schools, organizations, local and international school systems, churches, businesses, and other civic organizations. He has published several articles: *Urban Health*, "An Underplayed Need in Health Services and Podiatric Care," October 1974; Case Presentation, "Granuloma Cell Myoblastoma," 1976; and *Podiatry Yearbook*, "Clinical Laboratory Medicine," 1977–1978.

Dr. Todd is an ordained minister of the Gospel since 1977 and is an elder in the African Methodist Episcopal (AME) Church. In 1979, he served as pastor of several AME churches. He founded the Church of Hope Ministries (COHM) in 1985, a full gospel church, and later founded the Church of Hope Christian Academy, an educational facility for children. The Church of Hope Ministries, a non-denominational ministry, has also served as a chapter for "Promise Keepers." In 2014 he became a restorative practitioner.

The Church of Hope Ministries (whose services are streamed weekly) has a mission that consists of restorative principles and practices. In 2014, COHM graduated its first class of restorative justice practitioners (fourteen leaders in the church). COHM has a yearly Shoebox Ministry that has served one hundred youth in the community during Christmas holidays. The church collaborates with Perkerson Baptist Church and their youth ministry.

Dr. Todd presently serves as chief director of the specialty clinic at Southside Medical Center in Atlanta. He is the senior pastor at Church of Hope Ministries in Atlanta and is a retired major of the US Armed Forces. Dr. Todd's first marriage was to Nancy L. Martin, his second marriage was to Terumi Kuroshima, and his final marriage is with Roberta Williams Todd. He is the biological father of four sons (Frazier Ben Todd, Jr., Ado, Tobi, Emmanuel) and two daughters (Sandra, Angela). He has two sons by marriage (Jasper Williams III and Joseph L. Williams). He has a host of grand and great-grandchildren; Denaya, Levonne, Cynthia, Jennifer, Ronald, Brigitte, Frazier Ben III, Niah, Tamia, Ory, Kai, Akio, Kobi, Jaylin, Dayana, Dylan, Isaiah, Genesis, Jordan Phillip ,Jordan Josiah, Jordan, Jasper IV and Skyler.

Dr. Frazier Ben Todd, Sr., Timeline

1939-April 4, Born in Riverdale, Georgia

1941-42-Family moved to 708 Phillips Dr. (Thomasville Community of Atlanta)

1949- Family moved to 961 Turner Way (Thomasville Community of Atlanta)

1955- Family moved to 1810 Forest Park Rd. (Thomasville Community of Atlanta)

1956-Joined the United States Navy Reserve

1956- Featured in Local Atlanta newspaper "Mechanical Man, Robie"

1957-Graduated from Price Judson High School, Atlanta

1957- Featured in Atlanta Paper-introduced for playing with the Young Peoples Concert (Atlanta Symphony Orchestra)

1958- Married Nancy Martin

1958- Joined the U.S. Army, Ft. Chaffee, Army Basic Training

1958–1961- Chemical Command Ft. McClellan, Alabama. Student in the Chemical Corps, served as a specialist in chemical biological warfare. Ft. McClellan 296th Army Band Trumpet/Baritone Horn player

1958-1967 Primary Military Occupational Specialty (Medical Lab Specialist (U.S. Army)

1961- Ft. Bragg. NC, six months member of the Army Band

1961–1962- U.S. Army Medical Field Service School, Ft. Sam Houston, San Antonio, Texas. 67th Medical Group. Promoted to E-5 for outstanding contribution to the unit for the CBR training of the unit. Attended San Antonio University part-time.

1961–1963, Korea, chief laboratory director, 544th General Dispensary. Responsible for laboratory diagnosis and prevention of the spread of sexually transmitted diseases, malaria, and the prevention of bringing these diseases back to America.

1963–1964- San Francisco, Letterman General Hospital, Presidio, California, student in the 52-week Advanced Medical Laboratory Course.

1964–1965- Ft. Huachuca, Arizona, six months as a biological specialist in screening military personnel for infectious meningitis.

1965-Presidio General Dispensary, chief laboratory specialist

1965–1967- Theater of operations, Vietnam, 406th Medical Laboratory. Veterinary NCOIC (Non-commissioned officer in charge). Responsible for the safety of all food, water, and other consumable products used by military personnel.

1965 – First divorce (Nancy)

1966-Vietnam, 106th Hospital, promoted to E-6 NCOIC. Responsibilities included screening all military personnel returning to the U.S. for malaria.

1967-1972-Supervisor Clinical Laboratory Presbyterian Hospital, California

1968- Married Terumi Kuroshima.

1968- San Francisco, California. Supervisor, Pacific Medical Center night shift medical laboratory. Attended the University of San Francisco days.

1968–1972- California College of Podiatric Medicine, Samuel Merritt University. Graduated with DPM degree.

1969- Bachelor of Science Degree

1972–1973- Residency at Pacific Cost Hospital.

1972-1973-Assistant professor and lecturer at five of the College of Podiatric Medicine and Surgery centers (California)

1972- Doctor of Podiatric Medicine, California College of Podiatric Medicine

1973 - Dr. Todd & Associates Private Practice Atlanta, Georgia

1973- Southside Medical Center, Consultant

1974-Case Presentation, "Granuloma Cell Myoblastoma"

1974–1976- Fellowship Atlanta Hospital, foot and ankle surgery

1974, 2006, Private Practice (three locations in Georgia) including Foot and Ankle Surgical Center

1976-Published Article: Urban Health, "An Underplayed Need in Health Services and Podiatric Care"

1977-1979 Podiatry Yearbook, "Clinical Laboratory Medicine

1977- Southside Medical Center, Consultant1977- Ordained into the ministry

1979-Elder African Methodist Episcopal Church (AME)

1984, 1986 , Fellowship, Atlanta Hospital

1984-Major, US Army Reserve, Ft. Stewart, GA

1985- U.S. Army Reserve, Ft. McPherson, Atlanta. Also private practice in the grade of commissioned officer captain (0-3). Called to active duty yearly for training.

1985- Present (2019) Founder and Pastor of Church of Hope Ministries

1985-1991 Residency Director, Surgical Residency PSR24, Physicians and Surgeons Hospital, Atlanta, GA

1986, 1987, 1990-Uniformed Services University of the Health Sciences-Military Medicine Education Institute

1993- Promoted to the grade major (0-4), called to active duty for Desert Storm, Ft. Stewart, Georgia, Winn Army Hospital. Performed many surgical procedures on military personnel returning from the war zone.

1994- Second divorce (Terumi)

1995- Retired U.S. Army

1996-2006 CEO/Medical Director of Southwest Atlanta Ambulatory Foot and Ankle Surgical Center

2005- Married Roberta Williams

2006-Interdenominational Theological Center
Seminary Certificate

2006-present (2019) Fulltime Pastor COHM at Perkerson

2006-present, (2019), Fulltime Doctor of Podiatric Medicine
Southside Medical Center

2014-Completed training (Restorative Justice Institute of Atlanta, LLC) as a Restorative Justice Practitioner

ABOUT THE CO-AUTHOR, Janice Jerome

Janice Jerome is a native of Atlanta and the former Assistant Director for the University of Texas at Austin, Steve Hicks School of Social Work, the Institute of Restorative Justice and Restorative Dialogue (IRJRD). As a restorative practitioner, she is an expert trainer in the Texas Model of Restorative practices in education. She is a doctoral candidate for her Ph.D., in Transformative and Social Change. She received her master's degree in public administration and her bachelor's degree in computer science from Troy University, Troy Alabama. She has worked for the United States Department of Justice (USDOJ), Executive Office for Immigration Review (EOIR), Immigration Court in Miami, Florida and Atlanta, Georgia. She is the former Supervisor of Diversion / Intake for the Juvenile Court of Clayton County, Georgia. She is the founder of the Restorative Justice Institute of Atlanta, LLC. Janice founded "Spaces in the Rainbow," a free summer restorative workshop for youth and parents/caregivers to have meaningful conversations about violence at home, school, and in the community. Spaces in the Rainbow received a 2017 mini grant from the National Association for Community and Restorative Justice (NACRJ). In 2014, she collaborated with a local County Pretrial service organization to deliver a diversion workshop (bi-monthly) for those who are facing misdemeanor or felony charges related to theft. As of 2018, this workshop average 600 participants a year. In 2018, she established "Journey to the Heart" a holistic, restorative justice retreat for practitioners that is facilitated by pioneers in restorative. She is a contributor in the book *Colorizing Restorative*, published by Living Justice Press. She is the recipient of many awards including the 2015 Community and Leadership Restorative Justice Award from National Association of Community and Restorative Justice (NACRJ), the Romae Powell Award, and Director's Award from the Juvenile Courts Association of Georgia. She is a professional genealogist, mediator, anger management specialist, numismatics and paralegal. She is the mother of three and grandmother to one.